BREAKING & ENTERING

NEW AND SELECTED POEMS

Breaking & Entering

NEW AND SELECTED POEMS

1986 - 2021

Barbara Goldberg

THE WORD WORKS

WASHINGTON, D. C.

THE WORD WORKS
P.O. Box 42164
Washington, D.C. 20015
editor@wordworksbooks.org

Cover art:
"Tower," digital artwork by Catrin Welz-Stein
Cover design: Susan Pearce
Author photograph: Kevin Allen

LCCN: 2021942693
ISBN: 978-1-944585-46-4

ACKNOWLEDGMENTS

Special thanks to the editors of the following publications where some of the new poems in this book first appeared:

Beltway Quarterly: "Glass"
Innisfree: "After the War," "From the Top," "Outpost," "Harvest"
Moment Magazine: "By the Sea," "Memorial Day"
Nimrod: from "Writings From the Quattrocento"
Tikkun: "Furlough"

Some poems in this collection originally appeared in:

Berta Broadfoot and Pepin the Short: A Merovingian Romance by Barbara Goldberg. The Word Works & Porcupine's Quill © 1986
Cautionary Tales by Barbara Goldberg. Dryad Press © 1990
Marvelous Pursuits by Barbara Goldberg. Snake Nation Press © 1995
The Royal Baker's Daughter by Barbara Goldberg. Reprinted by permission of the University of Wisconsin Press. © 2008 by the Board of Regents of the University of Wisconsin System. All rights reserved. <https://uwpress.wisc.edu/books/4468.htm>
Kingdom of Speculation by Barbara Goldberg. Accents Publishing © 2015

I am grateful to The Word Works for publishing *Berta Broadfoot and Pepin the Short*, my first book, and some that followed, including *Scorched by the Sun: Poems by Moshe Dor*, *The Stones Remember: Native Israeli Poetry*, and the translations I selected as Series Editor of International Editions at The Word Works.

In memory of Aristides de Sousa Mendes

(1885-1954)

Save one, save generations.

CONTENTS

New Poems

Berta Broadfoot and Pepin the Short: A Merovingian Romance (1986)

Cautionary Tales (1990)

Marvelous Pursuits (1995)

The Royal Baker's Daughter (2008)

Kingdom of Speculation (2015)

*I prefer the absurdity of writing poems
to the absurdity of not writing poems.*

—Wislawa Szymborska

New Poems

FURLOUGH

I love to see those tall, lean, muscular men
with their clean-shaven heads and digital

watches toss their kids in the air. And I love
to see them drop, not weightless, but light

as grenades. This is how children learn that fear
can be fun. And fathers, that this too is hand

to hand combat. To cradle or kill—what story
do we tell ourselves to justify. That a *dunam*

of earth is worth dying for? That a child opening
his mouth with an *O* of pleasure overturns

everything? We grow like onions, our heads
buried in dirt. And we die like onions, face

down in a pot of boiling water. Gravity causes
all to fall down, and love, to hold things up.

BY THE SEA

How beautiful it is by the sea, even though
there is war in the air, even though there is always

war in the air, which makes people live
with a vengeance. On the roads fatalities

exceed those lost in battle. Children run
wild—all too soon they will sleep on stones

in the desert. In the sky planes fly lower
than you would think possible, low enough

to wipe your plate clean. There's an airport
less than a mile from the promenade

and the sea, the beautiful sea, duplicitous
in nature, licking your lips and wrapping

her salty arms around your neck until you
succumb to the whirling rapture of the deep.

OUT OF RANGE

Three seconds after we miss the turn
the iPhone goes dark and the GPS
stops talking. It seems we have strayed
into a foreign country. Streets smell

more pungent and doors stand out,
a vivid blue, but license plates are still
the same orange. Intruders have been here
before—there's the hotel that once

was a palace built by a pasha for
his four wives. And look at those
palm trunks pockmarked by bullets.
We are not to blame, just travelers

without a map, wary of the locals.
They hate us. We feel it seep through
the windows. Anything is possible.
No road wide enough for a U-turn.

OUTPOST

They built the high places of Baal in the valley of the son of Hinnom.
—2 Chron. 28.3

An Arab boy in blue flip flops galloping bareback the length
of the valley, back and forth, over and over, cigarette clenched
between his teeth, cell phone pressed to his ear, faster, faster,
he's spurring the horse on now, steering him up the rim
of the valley and suddenly out into noonday traffic, out
of time, out of place, cars grinding to a halt, the rhythmic
clop clop of hooves pounding tarmac.
                                                                From the terrace
of a pricey café overlooking the valley I see dry trampled grass,
a small grove of olive trees, black-draped women gossiping
in the shade, children wrestling, can almost smell warm hummus
with *foule*, pickled turnips, *mujaddara*, this valley still called Gai
Ben Hinom, Tophet, Gehenna,
                                            where children were offered
to the great god Moloch, the stench of charred flesh, of burnt offal
pervading the valley for centuries. To the left, the old walls of the city,
to the right, a dusty white village crouched on a hillock. I am eating
a thin crust margherita one leg
                                            outstretched the other dangling
dangling over the edge

MEMORIAL DAY
Yom Hazikaron

Eleven sharp. Sirens wail, cleave
the heart of the country. Everything
stops. People get out of their cars

and stand at attention. The dead stir
underfoot. Everyone knows someone.
Say *Chinese farm*, say *Budapest*,

and you're back in a tank, back
in the Sinai, back in hell. Taste it
in olives, in sesame seeds—they stick

in your gullet. Smell it when you fill up.
And who wouldn't be running on empty,
lash out at random? Everyone knows

someone. When three stars appear
in the sky it's over. Fireworks explode,
punctuate the night, proclaim the joyful

founding of the State. Grief falls back
in the black hole of your pocket. Tomorrow
flags and barbecues and cake.

HARVEST

whose sky   whose clouds   whose bleached

white sun   whose thorns   whose hills   whose

sniper   whose troops   whose trucks   whose

trees   whose olives   whose stones   whose land

PENELOPE'S SONG

The gods need ample playing fields
for their displays, their quarrels staged
through intermediaries. Gray-eyed Athena

stole my husband for his cleverness,
called him her 'chamelion.' For years
I wove, by night unraveled, my heart

balanced on a single thread. In a flash
his first step back on rocky ground she
transformed him from king to beggar

dressed in dusty rags. All this to foil
the suitors. They were so fooled they threw
their pots at him. He slew them in the end.

It all hinged on the stringing of the bow.
Athena's foe? Poseidon, god of the sea.
Mine was loneliness, the air I breathed.

*

He used to call me his stubborn child, a child
who took perverse delight in saying no. But that's
not so. I was full grown even then, the child, in fact

our own. He said I was stiff-necked from being kept
on too short a leash. So when I tasted in our bed
that first bite of sweet, I went wild. Wild as the branches

of an olive tree. *No, I don't want to rest, no, I don't
want to sit. No, I don't want to weave.* Went wild
with no. But no now stands him well as 100 brazen

suitors mill about and gorge themselves on plums
and pigs. His. They would eat him out of house
and home. And throne. This "child" is steadfast

in her no. In her refusal. For neither I, nor my
position, nor Telemachus, the rightful heir, will fall
without a fight. A pleasure, then, unraveling at night.

*

A pleasure, then, unraveling at night, allow
the muscles of the face go slack, relax.
Some say I wither on the vine. Sometimes

I want to take them all, each scheming one
and hurl them in the wine-dark sea. Do
what cannot be undone. Let fate decree.

Our faithful dog is going blind. He yawns because
his world has turned monochrome. His tongue
unfurls and licks my palm, the pungent flavors

of dyed wool. And skin. His life swims out against
the tide. I could go on. And on. As Odysseus
sailed on without a parting word. In the telling

they will say he won his wars, can call himself
a man. But if he lives he grieves to leave this child
alone. Wanting, as he does, me for his own.

*

As Athena wants him, for her own. Although
they call her fair, they do not know her greed.
Ten thousand times more she wants to quell

Poseidon—because he ravished her by sea.
His mistake was thinking her submission
permanent. And would have been had she not

been a god. What is it, then, to be a god, to count
on immortality? Does one cease to be lured
by song/refrain, but long for other melodies?

*

No mention of a feature that my self defines, not
gray-eyed like Athena, nor like my husband
versatile. And what do gray eyes signify but

gray like ashes or the feathers of an owl? Yet
Odysseus chose me—the blank, the cipher, naught,
mere shade to Calypso's majesty. He calls me quiet,

downplays my stubborn streak, his own
thirst for home. He dreamt a fate heroic, one
only death allows, therefore no god can have it,

a choice not many men would make save one
most vain. Something a little extra for a son
to glorify. Would I have chosen thus, spurning

life eternal? Coupled with remaining youthful
in every way? Yet to see Odysseus grow old,
indifferent to Dawn's shining ringlets. And then

a timeless time alone. Life is fraught with choices.
Perhaps I too would choose to die if one composed
a song for me, the Quiet Penelope.

FROM THE TOP

He placed the metronome in the sink and the Mozart
on the toilet because it was the one room
in the house with no rug and the acoustics were
outstanding. Every day he'd emerge for Oprah,
his one sure way to unwind. He was a boy
of seventeen, a young man, really, a prodigy
on the clarinet playing his instrument with tenderness
and clarity. He tells how first while playing
Schumann he heard this one arpeggio—*broken
chord in the manner of the harp*—and was transported.

How can something broken sound celestial? In the echo
chamber of the soul reverberates all that's brittle, bruised
and bitter, bankrupt and foreclosed. And yet—to be
transported in this time of static, time of woe, when what
consoles is down to earth, straight talk from the haloed
heart, *broken chord in the manner of the harp*.

GLASS

A man here is known as the King
of Porn: just enter your fantasy online
and a few minutes later there's a knock
at your door. In this way a poor émigré
became a billionaire. As for himself,
his own obsession was to go legit, be
a mover and shaker in the art world.

And thus it happened. He launched
a magnificent gallery in a magnificent
building where he displayed his own
collection of glass, glass sculpture,
glass installations, and many sold

for hundreds of thousands of dollars.
Soon his gallery was flooded by more
visitors than any museum in the country.
Stationed throughout were private guards
who lent a certain caché. And who

wouldn't stare at an enormous glass pear, or
the trunk of a ficus that seemed fashioned
of wood. Tucked away in a small dark room
was the jewel in the crown: a chandelier
hanging eye-high with chubby angels
and ruby red devils captured midflight.

It was marvelous, entrancing, out
of this world. If you walked down a corridor
still under construction you'd find at the end
looming larger than life a translucent

tombstone, but instead of a name, a mirror
reflecting your own image. How strange
that a man who could clearly see through
the crystal heart of desire could be so
possessed by what is so easily broken.

MARILYN

Had it been me I never would have
chosen her, too blond, too white, too

drop-dead gorgeous. Not to mention
her voice—breathy and hesitant. I guess

some men like that. Luckily for Marilyn
I'm not a man. Now take Audrey Hepburn,

petite, spiked bangs, French twist, her taste
for wit, someone I could grow into. So many

girls like to make themselves stupid, or lose
on purpose, like this girl in college, also blond,

also stacked, she could spin a thousand angels
on the head of a pin, but at parties she'd drink

too much and act dumb. The boys, she said, ate
it up. I wouldn't even want a guy like that

who wouldn't know how to spar or crack
a joke, who'd simply ache to dive head-first

into her décolletage and sleep in the pillowy
softness of her flesh. I preferred those

who hoarded secrets, little treasures buried
like truffles, deep in the underbelly of the earth.

HIS MOTHERLAND

I know he will return to you, a broken man, scarcely
a man at all. Others can't escape your clutch, like Rafi
wed to avocado groves, four walls he does not own,
a walkway labored over, brick by wretched brick
and the daughter he did not father, a bad seed
from the start. Farewell Eulalia and Barcelona.
Grief takes root under the burning sun of Ga'ash.

Today another farewell by fax—Margalit for Chile
and the grown sons who hardly know her, farewell
the press and the love of a proud man. "Terminal,"
he writes, as all is that does not die young. But you,
you will have him in the end. His sweetest songs are lifted
from my lips, where seasons pass over and nothing
is sacred. I eat the flesh, you the bones.

AFTER THE WAR

It was a Czech film and the lead was a dead ringer
for my uncle, same full cheeks, almond eyes, same
slicked-back hair. There he was, my uncle, on screen,
larger than life. The movie was made after the war
and had a happy ending, our hero reclaiming his fortune,
his life. My uncle also survived, spared by the angel
of death, Mengele himself, fastidious, spick and span,
spotless in white. *Step to the right*, he said, because

my uncle was young, and strong, and knew how
to weld. I met my uncle when I was four, after
the camps, after the year he spent in a Swiss sanitarium
to put on weight, after the judge at Ellis Island
changed his name from Pavel to Paul, Briess
to Brennan, the "Irishman from Prague." He seemed
to live a charmed life after the war, used the cash
my father gave him to play the market, married

money, became the life of the party with his endless
repertoire of jokes, which he couldn't stop telling.
After my father died he embezzled money from
my mother, his sister, but she forgave him, "after all
he went through," which he never talked about until
he was dying, and even then only the funny stories—
the bunkmate who threw shoes at him after liberation,
Here, he said, *you saved me, now you wear them, they're killing*

my feet. What if that dashing movie star and my uncle
really had been twins, identical, indulged with sweets
before dissection by Uncle Josef, who also survived
to make a new life for himself in Brazil, marrying
his brother's wife, living to a ripe old age, then dying
of a massive stroke while swimming? He was a doctor.
He should have known better than to plunge into the ocean
so soon after the noonday meal, and on a full stomach.

WRITINGS FROM THE QUATTROCENTO

*From letters and journal entries of Tommasa di Benedetto
Malefici, wife of Paolo Uccello (1397-1475), Renaissance
painter and sculptor best known for Perspective Theory.*

The Birth Day of Our Lord, 1425

My Lord, you have gone
far. I see it by your letter
from San Romano. I am pleased
the hunt goes well. Here
in my chambers, I dip
the needle through the green
silk of your robe.

Feast of the Epiphany, 1425

My dear, it rains. Days
are like thick gloves covering
my fingers. I have not the heart
to sew. And yet, there is much
to do. Adalfa has taken to stealing
eggs from the guinea hen. Lorenzo
lacks your skill with the horses.
They balk and grow fretful. I am not
with child, as we had hoped.
I beg you to be patient.
I am still young and in good
health. Your brother tries
to taunt you about your manhood.
He has always been jealous of you,
the firstborn. His Marta is like a sow,
dropping piglets as though they were eggs.

Candlemas, 1425
Paolo. The nights are hard.
I cannot sleep for longing.
And yet, if I lie perfectly
still, I sometimes hear the tunes
you used to play within my font.

Shrove Tuesday, 1426
Just yesterday Ghiberti
sent word that your services
are required. Yet another
set of gates, this time
of Paradise. Do you suppose
that these will also take
twenty-five years like the North
Baptistry Doors? I once asked him
if he had not grown bored
with his doors, with quatrefoils
enough for any lifetime. Do you know
what he said? "My doors are
entryways to the spirit." "But Signor,"
I replied. "Your doors are so
magnificent one never wishes
to open them. Those doors keep
people out." I was feeling
gay that day. This was before
little Paolo's fever.

Whitsunday, 1426

My husband. I know
you still grieve.
I know the sight of me
is loathsome to you.
You see in me his eyes,
his chin. He was dear
to me too. Especially
today. One year ago
he was baptized in
white robes. What is it
you need to hunt for in that
thicket? Surely not
the Holy Ghost in the lost
limb of a tree.

Journal Entry, All Saint's Day, 1427

To him it is a game.
I could crack an egg, or
pull my hair, it's all
the same. He looks up
with a baffled mien
before returning with ardent
concentration to his compass
and protractor. He maps out
a multitude of intersecting
lines, and shifts an angle here,
an angle there, in the wild
hope that all lines
will meet in the infinite distance.
I know he wracks his brain—
how can the appearance of near
and far be rendered on a flat

plane? This intricate quest
absorbs him, keeps him young
and buoyant. When we dine
I feel his years fall upon me
in the candlelight. After soup
and fish and flan the lines
around my eyes and mouth define themselves
more deeply. If he raised his glance
to really look at me he'd see how near
and far are merely metaphor of present,
past and future. Ah, but his realm is space
and all its variations, while mine is time.
The two realms intersect, of course: for instance,
when he went far, I ached for his return.
Now that he's here I feel a greater
distance. And when he strokes my breast
I know he thinks of orthogons and where
to plot the vanishing point. My Paolo
truly serves a higher Master. But I am young
to renounce the pleasures of the flesh, once
having known its mad trembling. I should be
grateful for his fidelity. He does not cast
an eye at other comely women. If only
I were an ordinary chalice to be analyzed!
He would view me with greater fascination
and I would be held in dearer regard.

Journal Entry, Childermas, 1428
I hear the hoofbeats so I know
he's gone. My faith, I'm red
all over. He caused my blood
to rise by his knowing look,
his insolent smile. And thus

he struts before my husband,
his older brother, with such
an air of cheerful malice.
It's as though he lifts
my skirts and slips
right in, at home
in the darkness of my inner
soul. But no, I cannot
even think that way. Soul
I said, but I believe
the soul to be pure spirit,
not cognizant of heartbeats
or that slow spreading warmth
between my thighs and yes,
I feel his touch, his knowing
root inside me, rocking
to our own sweet music.
And nights I've lain awake
and felt his lips, his cock
just so, just so, dear Lord,
I've always been a gentle woman
but this is new, new and strange.
I must be confused, to have
such shameful thoughts with
no sense of shame. I must
find useful work to do. Alas
there are no children and I've
been warned against another
misadventure. After little
Paolo's burial I did not wish
to live—another sin
and so I fortified myself
but truly against my will.
It is written, *This too
shall pass*. Shall
this pass? For the everlasting
fate of my soul I pray it does.

But if it should be that
after death there is only darkness,
then I will swallow with
bitter rue, bitter rue,
all that I could have done
but did not do.

Feast of Fools, 1455
Cara Franca. Have you heard
the scandal concerning Fra Filippo Lippi?
I have no quarrel with his painting.
He was appointed Chaplain of the convent
in Prato. It is said he shares himself
with the nun Lucrezia (how that name
still causes my heart to ache!),
her sister Spinetta and five
other nuns! And more, Lucrezia
has already presented him
with a son. Why God should favor
such a heinous coupling
remains to me a mystery.
How my heart swells
at your wondrous news!
Of course, travel is out
of the question now. You must be sure
to only listen to harmonious music
and to avoid garlic and rapscallions!
The joy that awaits you!

Maundy Thursday, 1456
Little Franca, poor Franca, I weep
with you at your loss. I know the way
you feel like the inside of my mouth.
I'm glad you find solace in the garden.
Paolo has found his solace in perspective

and endless diagrams of distance. He jokes
of his obsession, calls it "my sweet mistress."
Often he forgets to enter my bedchambers.
He makes light of it, but you must know
how it pains me. The peppery taste
still lingers. I find some measure
of peace in our chapel. Franca, it seems
mere days ago that we sat at Mama's
rosewood desk and built that soaring
house of cards.

from

Berta Broadfoot and Pepin the Short: A Merovingian Romance

(1986)

CHARACTERS:

Princess Berta of Hungary, known historically as Berta Broadfoot, possibly because she was clubfooted, daughter of Queen Blancheflor and King Floire of Hungary.

King Pepin the Short of France, son of Charles Martel. First King of the Franks to be appointed by the Pope 753 A.D. Marries Princess Berta in 741 A.D.

Carloman, Pepin's older brother, a brave knight who enters a monastery under mysterious circumstances, renouncing his land and inheritance.

Margiste, trusted handmaiden to Queen Blancheflor. Accompanies Berta to France in order to see her safely married and become her personal servant.

Aliste, Margiste's daughter. Illegitimate daughter of King Floire of Hungary. Bears a great physical resemblance to Berta, save for the size of her feet.

Holy Hermit, lives in the forest of Le Mans.

Pilgrim

Soothsayer

Le Maistre Des Haultes Oeuvres, Executioner to King Pepin.

King Pepin the Short of France and Princess Berta of Hungary became the parents of Charlemagne.

PROLOGUE: MARGISTE REVEALS

But listen. It is an old tale.
A maiden is switched for a maiden
in the bridal bed. In the dark
who can tell? A man is a man
and humps for his own release.
The dark is dark. Does he look
at the feet? Only a mother knows
her child by the feet. Berta,
Debonaire, was quick to believe
that Pepin would come with a knife.
I disrobed Aliste in her stead.
And Berta, gagged by a rope, smothered
in cloth, was led to the lonely
dark forest of Mans. We thought all
was well. Aliste chirped like a bird,
levied taxes on pepper, cumin and wax.
We should have fled to Sicily.
Pepin twists my thumbs with screws.
I confess! I confess all! Even
the dagger, even the poison, no regrets!
A great fire is kindled with thorns.

BERTA REMEMBERS CHILDHOOD GAMES
WITH ALISTE

At the edge of the forest pretending
we were pigs snuffling for acorns
under the oak trees, under an oak

she wrestled me to the ground, pricked
my thumb with a thistle. We are sisters,
she whispered. Laughing

I called her my wild carnelian cherry.
She lifted my skirts and whispered,
Sister. Bloodroot. Little radish.

BERTA REFLECTS ON HER WEDDING DAY

The Hawks

The King is beside himself. From the Abbott
a wedding gift: six white hawks, miraculous!
He races to find a red cloth lure, stuffed
with chicken hearts. The birds, released,
attack the lure, hearts fall out, disappear.

The falconer covers the hawks with leather
hoods, fastens the claws' golden rings inscribed
with these words: "I belong to the King."

I saw it once, a man accused of stealing
birds. Ravenous beaks allowed to feast
on human flesh, his bloodied chest. I hear
it still, piercing screams, as bells retreat
to open sky. Off to one side, the hawk-dealer
stood, yawning and satisfied.

The Tapestry

The Abbott has not forgotten me: a sumptuous
tapestry of the Lady in the Garden. Her
handmaiden kneels at her feet in shimmering
emerald green, as Aliste kneels before me now,
painting my toenails and chattering.

I have ordered the tapestry hung from the East
window. Griffon and deer blaze up in silk,
perfect and diminutive. I could lie down
in that crimson field, bare my breast
to the crimson sky. And all around
the ripening smells of apples and muscatel.

Reflections

I never cared for birds, neither *oiseaux*
de poing, nor *oiseaux de leure*. I prefer
the lyre, its measured notes, to songbirds.
Yet I adore my Pekinese, fidelity based
on love, not the scent of bloodied quail.
What nature of beast my new husband?

For sixteen years I have been your daughter.
Soon I shall be wife and Queen. I am drawn
to the Lady, target for the enchanted arrow.
They say the arrow never misses its mark,
can reach game from extraordinary distances.
Birds of prey see a hare's whiskers from
extraordinary heights. Mother, how can I
explain? It's not that my heart didn't race
when Pepin took my hand, but rather
I feel an extraordinary distance
from the only self I have ever known.

ALISTE CONSIDERS HER POSITION

Who was there to turn to when I found
his morning gift, a handsome brooch
encrusted with pearls, on my pillow?
Him? Not him, no morning gift, pink
and strutting, boasting of the seed
he felt spring from him with the force
of ten thousand steeds. When he forced
himself on me, pink, boastful, bent
to suckle like a piglet in his greed,
who was there? He threw his head back,
shouted, boasting of his seed, my morning
gift, and who was there to turn to? I set
my lips in imitation of a smile, spread
my limbs like any sow, but who was there?
Could I proclaim, pink and strutting, "This.
This is who I am, your morning gift, servant
girl who cannot sign her name. And do you
love her still? Would you leave a gift,
a morning gift, a handsome brooch, on her
pillow?" Who was there, who, to turn to?

Not Mother, hopping about with glee, fingers
greasy from palace meat. She pokes my ribs
and cackles, "We fooled him, eh? We two
make quite a team." We two make quite a team
when, hankering for all I've lost, I think
of home and sister and the poor dumb sheep
I used to shear. Sister. Sister. Poor
dumb sheep I used to shear. Berta and I
once laughed ourselves asleep. I shuddered
when I saw her heart, darkly gleaming in
Mother's palm. She hopped about with glee,
then tossed it down her throat. "There,"
she said, "That's done," her fingers greasy

from the meat. And poked my ribs, while I,
dumb sheep, play the part of Queen. Berta
and I, we could have made a team. And laughed
ourselves asleep. I've thought of claiming
defect of consent, *diriment impediment*, but
Mother would be lost for good, poor sheep.
Since there is no one human I can turn to,
I turn with more than human need to the feel
of silk, darkly gleaming, next to my skin.

LETTER FROM PEPIN TO CARLOMAN

My beloved brother,
at last a moment between petitions
to take up pen and write to you,
who are dearest in my heart. I grieve
today because my horse, most faithful
companion in hunt and battle, has fallen,
not by sword or arrow, but from ignominious
disease. When I saw the blood flow from his lips,
I myself thrust in the sword, and tears flowed
from my eyes. He cannot be replaced, but
I have entrusted Gaudiocus with forty sous
to buy the palomino stallion I so admired
at Ardennes. I suppose in time I shall
be able to mount him with a flying leap,
in the meantime, I mourn. As I mourn
your absence. To think of your poring
over manuscripts when once you pierced
many a helmet, broke many a *hauberk*,
cut off many an enemy's head. How valiant
you were, second to none! I have never
understood your decision, to renounce
all that, as well as the sparrow hawks
and the falcons. Not to mention maidens
in their first bloom!

Berta is well, although, just like a woman,
she does nothing but speak of bolts of silk
from Pavia. A wife costs dearly, Carloman,
to keep them gentle. Last week nothing less
than an otter cloak could unpinch her lips,
loosen her thighs. And now she croons to me
morning and night about silk, silk.

My liver troubles me. I find a spoonful
of honey, vinegar, mustard and ten grains
of pepper soothing. A recent diversion
was a visit from the Ambassador of Baghdad.
A hunt with full clamor for aurochs. How
the Asiatics fear wild oxen! Heudris,
my younger son, stamped his feet until
I consented to let him watch from a hillock.
But Rainfrois, I fear, shall never be a hunter.
He clings to his mother well past the age
in such matter. She dotes on him, fosters
his unmanliness. Remember when I faced that
lion, disemboweled him in a twinkling with my sword?
How proud our mother was! Would that all my time
could be spent hunting and fighting, but alas
there are always affairs of state and endless
details to attend to—appeasing the Pope,
our half-brother Grifo a constant thorn
in my side. He tries to incite the Saxons.
And can you imagine? A mere hogshead of oats
costs a whole denier.

Dear brother—do not become ascetic.
Consent to warm yourself and to bathe.
I imagine you with a parchment
under your arm, a cowl over your head.
Remember me in your prayers.

BERTA SURVIVES HER ORDEAL

After the ground shook with the thud
of hooves, and they left me trembling
in my white chemise, rain began to fall,
whipped by an an icy wind. I stumbled through
the forest, tripping over slippery stones,
my arms scratched by low-hanging branches.
Lightning flashed, revealed an opening—
I darted down one path, then another,
but soon was lost in a maze of trees.
How dense those woods were, and how forsaken.
Owls hooted from the treetops, wolves howled
in the distance. "Saint Denis!" I cried out,
"I am lost! Saint Catherine! Save me!"
I sped wearily on, my dress torn and ragged,
until I found a hollow spot, laid my sorrows
at god's feet, and chilled and lost as I was,
I slept.

When I awoke, blue from cold, I prayed, "Sir God,
show me where to go and henceforth I will be humble.
I will never tell who I am, not that I am the daughter
of Hungary, nor the wife of France. Grant that I
may keep my maidenhood. And may Margiste suffer
a horrible death!" God led me to a holy hermit
who showed me the path to Simon and Constance.

Sooner than I like to think, life became quite ordinary.
The ordinary crust of bread, the ordinary courtesies.
Those sturdy, upright people accepted me, a stranger
with no trace of past. They marveled at my modesty,
while inwardly I longer for throne and kingly caresses.
Daily I read in my psalter. How glorious the illuminations,
the Madonna's robes a brilliant blue from lapis lazuli,
and carmine from the little ilex beetle.

From my Book of Hours, the haymakers in June
formed a backcloth to the gaudy lives of nobles
making love in May. Years passed. I began to sense
the power that comes from guarding a secret vow long
past its earthly usefulness. By granting all to God,
I maintained sovereignty over my own soul.

Praise God in all His generosity. The more
arduous the keeping of my vow, the more regal
and full of circumstance my rule.

THE HOLY HERMIT TURNS BEAUTY AWAY

There came a time in my life when all
I craved was order: the exact dimension
of the Earth's diameter, facts a stay
against famine and war. The moon
is 39 times smaller than our planet,
the sun 166 times larger. To be sure
it is difficult to speak of the stars,
so far away that if a stone were thrown
from one, it would take 100 years to land
near this hut (at the rate of 74¼ miles
per hour). If I were to walk at the rate
of 25 miles per day, it would take me
7,157½ years to reach the stars. Less
time is needed for a good soul after death
to arrive at Heaven—under half-an-hour
to be precise.

And this only speaks of distance.
What of the beaver who severs its testicles
in order to escape the hunter? So I
(a holy hermit) would triumph over temptation.
Consider the fate of the antelope—captured
when its needle-sharp horns become entangled
in a bush. "Beauty," I told her, "I can let
no fiend in, neither in summer nor winter."
She was the Devil come to tempt me, what else
was Beauty doing in these leafy woods? I passed
her a piece of bread through the wicket, told her
the path to the home of Simon the Sheriff. God
is my judge. I must beware the Infernal Hunter
who seeks to impale the souls of men.

THE PILGRIM STATES HIS CASE

I am a pilgrim in search of wonders. I have seen fragments from the Holy Cross and tattered bits from the Holy Coat. I was at Mozac when the chapel was so crowded that women wailed as though in childbirth. I escaped with my life by walking on the worshippers' heads.

The best prostitutes are to be found near chapels. Last night a prostitute tricked me into going to her home with the oldest ploy in the world: she claimed to know me from childhood.

The life of a pilgrim is too great a hardship for a man with family. It is best to travel alone.

My beloved wife is barren. That is why I visit so many towns and worship the remains of the apostles.

Yes, I know the recipe for maleficium. Doesn't everyone? One mixes a potion from fern roots, willow leaves, rue, gillyflower seeds and saffron. But I have never administered such a potion to one with child.

I slept at the hostelry last night. It was crowded with pilgrims come to visit the boy's grave. Tomorrow is Good Friday, the anniversary of his miraculous death.

Last night I spent some time in the tavern. The wine here is unusually sour.

The laws in this town are just. There are allowances made if one commits certain crime while in one's cups.

The sheriff Simon invited me to his home last night. During the day I had helped him catch a poacher.

There are many lovely maidens in this town. Not just the three who reside with Simon and Constance.

Most of the women in this town are old, with flesh like pudding. I have a distaste for women who sprout hair from moles on their chins.

I have thought of becoming a monk. The rules of chastity would be easier for me to obey than the rule of silence.

Simon's adopted daughter Berta was rude to me when I complimented her on her embroidery. Aiglente and Ysobel were happy to launder my shirt. No, I never pulled off her headdress.

Life in some towns is so tedious. Great crowds will gather just to see a dog run frantically with a pan tied to his tail.

I have been to the Island Taprobane, the true terrestrial Paradise. Each year it was two winters and two summers.

You are fortunate to have such reliquaries in this town. They ensure revenue for the populace and many pilgrims who will dazzle you with tales from afar while you sit in the safety of your chair.

How does a town begin? Four crosses are placed at the cardinal points. Trace out the limits, build church, town hall, market place, squares, streets. Then give it a name: Neuville, Villeneuve, Neufchateau, Villefranche.

I did not lift the maiden's skirt. I did not lift it to the calf. I did not lift it to the knee. I did not force her to remove her garments. I am more tempted by sweet cakes than women.

I was with a prostitute last night, as I told you.

I was at the tavern last night, as I told you.

I merely had dinner with Simon and Constance last night as I told you.

It's true I travel widely, but I have a wife and six children in the town of Villefranche.

I mostly reluctantly agree to pay a fine of forty sous. Perhaps I did touch her headdress, but only as a gesture of friendship. I most emphatically did not touch her elsewhere.

I plan to leave immediately. Please accept my donation of forty sous for the care of the reliquary. A cup of water would be most appreciated. I am not used to the wine in this town.

THE SOOTHSAYER INTERPRETS
BLANCHEFLOR'S DREAM

The Dream

In this dream the dreamer
knows she is dreaming. Holds a wide-
toothed comb in her hand. Soft
thump at door. Enter a bear.
She pulls comb through dark fur.
Strong odor of musk, honey,
cloves. Dreamer sings lulla,
lullaby, go to sleep my plump
sweet. Bear sucks on paw.
Paw becomes raking claw.
Tears cheek, rips right arm,
begins to gnaw at dreamer's
rib-cage. Scatters bones on floor.
Dreamer finds mirror. Torso
a carcass. Right arm dangles
from its socket. Face half-
gone. Bear sees bear. Mirror
mirror. Bear bear. Thump thump.

The Interpretation

I bind phylacteries with ribbons
to my arms, with cords to my legs.
Combine letters of dreamer's name.
I climb to the rooftop, pay heed
to the direction of smoke. Study
the sky. Make note that moon
in fourth quarter. Omen of death.
Comet appears in sign of Scorpio.
Open book at random. Scrutinize
all data. Interpretation: extreme
danger to dreamer's daughter. Long
voyage required. Dreamer pulls hair
in lamentation. There is no pleasure
to such work.

ALISTE SPEAKS WITH DOUBLE TONGUE

I couldn't stand   this fact: they were torturing her
I couldn't sit   I could hear her shrieks
I paced, a wild thing   she couldn't save me now
until he stormed   but who was there, who
in my bedchamber   to save me, strike me down.
struck me down. How   How could I, over and over
could I after all   save her? I was her prisoner
our nights together in bed caught in deceit. I couldn't
grabbing me, scratching my face protect her, she couldn't protect
my breasts, his tears staining me, unbearably alone. I clung to
his cheeks. "Lost!" he cried clinging to the bedpost. "Mother!" I cried
and I did fear him   for Mother. The flames
ardent in rage, rising,   the smell of scorched flesh
I think he must   never never cease to
love that girl   blame her, her ambition
departing now on horseback now reduced to ash.

MARGISTE PROTESTS

If I were a man they would sing
of my daring, call me Margiste
the Bold. No lioness did more
for her cub. Gladly I'd give my
scarlet hose for a song
of my daughter, Aliste of the
Narrow Feet. Instead they sing of
Bert aus Grans Pies, Bertha
Broadfoot, Berta the Debonaire.
Why should *she* have been Queen of France,
were both girls not blonde, not fair?
Both dimpled, both winsome, both
mantled with golden hair? Both sired
by Hungarian King Floire? (His wife,
Blancheflor, so noble, so pure, she
always gave to a fault to the poor.)
Berta was Highborn, Aliste a mere
serving girl. Yet for eight years she
played Queen to Pepin the Short. He
was well-satisfied. My cousin Tibert
(incompetent dolt) swore that Berta
was slain. I piss on Berta! I piss on her
big feet! Fooled by a pig's heart!
Burned for bearing a girl with narrow
feet! I don't care a mint leaf
what Pepin calls me now ("old hag, the
Antichrist"). He once covered my daughter
from evening till dawn. Let them kindle for
me a great fire with thorns!

LE MAISTRE DES HAULTES OEUVRES
REPORTS TO THE KING

As the King's Sworn Tormentor, I am bound to
inform you of events that transpired
to the old woman you placed in my charge.
As you instructed, the following preparatory
Tortures were administered: the usual twisting of
thumbs with screws, during which hot eggs were
placed under the armpits. According
to your fancy, goats were led in to avidly lick
her feet, which had been doused in salt water.
This proved a most effective agony. Confession
was immediately forthcoming.

You decreed her crime a capital offense:
execution by fire. The stake was erected
in the designated spot, the northern section of
the marketplace. The pile was carefully
prepared, as per the most efficient design:
layers of straw and wood were alternated to the
victim's height. Pains were taken
to leave a free space round the stake
and a passage that led to it. The victim's
body hair was shaved. She was stripped of
her clothing and dressed in a shirt
smeared with sulphur. She walked through the
narrow opening to the pile's center.
Ropes and chains tightly bound her to
the stake. Faggots and straw
were thrown into empty spaces until she
was entirely covered. The fire
was lit from all sides at once. Her body was
slowly devoured by flames.

When it was possible, I approached the center
of the burning pile, scooped a few ashes
in a shovel, sprinkled them into the air.
I am your most trusted servant, am always
at your disposal.

LE MAISTRE DES HAULTES OEUVRES
REPORTS TO ALISTE

Lady, I accept with thanks your gift
of one hundred gold sous. It is not
that I am without means: *havage*
from every load of grain, taxes
on sales of herring and watercress,
the fine of five sous levied on stray
pigs, which is my due. There are rents
from shops and stalls surrounding the
pillory. Still, here an odium
is attached to my craft. Not so
in other lands. Here, I am forced
to wear a yellow coat. The Chancellor
threw my letters of appointment
under the table, a token of contempt.
Such is the source of my discontent.
Consider the services I provide:
execution by fire, sword, mechanical
force; administration of quartering,
the wheel, the fork, the gibbet,
drawing, spiking, cutting of ears,
dismembering, flogging, the pillory.
And my other services to the community:
one can buy fat from me of culprits
who have been hung, the medicinal value
of which is well-known. My expertise
in the setting of limbs. Enough.
I shall use your gift to apply
for a position in Bavaria, where
I will be treated with respect.
Now to assure you that your gift enabled
death to be swift and painless. I
placed a large and pointed bar
amongst the faggots opposite the
stake, breast high. This bar

impaled the unfortunate woman,
delivering a mortal blow directly
after the fire was lit. Praise God I
could spare her suffering.

BERTA CONVERSES WITH GOD

Sir God, I was not prepared
for this, intemperate love
annihilating all restraint.
Here I lie in rose-water,
chewing seeds of anise!

After years of baking barley
bread, gathering twigs for
firewood, an ever-present
line of dirt was etched
beneath my fingernails.

No pallet on the beaten
floor, but massive bed
with silken sheets, far
from pleasures that I found
in sacred vows, embroidery.

I am greedy for the black figs
which are his eyes, the flowering
almond smoothness of his skin,
that pale pink mushroom, his
manhood in a state of rest.

When our energies are spent,
no strength to even lift
a wrist, I turn to lick
the salt-sweat from the
hollow of his neck.

I know not if it be night
or day, or if the moon be full
or new, but only that I am
most blessed when he drinks
the warm wine of my womanhood.

from

Cautionary Tales

(1990)

CAUTIONARY TALES

In the woods
are these things:

fingers of madmen
nimble and quick
playing cat's cradle
with ropes meant for strangling

a great horned owl
in the treetop
the soul of a Chippewa
caught in its throat

a sidewinding snake
rubbing its scales
jaws unhinged
hungry for neckbones

quicksand, though no one
knows where exactly

There are stories our children tell us
to keep us from wandering.

THE WOODCUTTER

The woodcutter's hut
squats in the forest
like a mushroom.

He lives like a monk
and waits for the grim
commands.

He hardly gets to his
chopping. He is given
many tasks:

Once, there was a Queen
who had a hunger
for daughter's heart.
She called upon the woodcutter
to perform this delicate surgery.

Instead he returned
with the heart of a wild boar,
which the Queen salted,
never tasting the difference.

Again, in the cottage hard
by the edge of the wood
he deftly dissected
a rapacious wolf.
It was as easy as
slicing liver.

A girl and her grandmother
hopped out like little frogs.

At night he comes home
from his labors. His heart
is empty of desire.
He has a simple supper
of bread and cheese.
He hones his ax.

TEETH

We all live in dread of our teeth
falling out into our cupped palms.
We pray for our teeth, clattering
in the bone chamber of the skull.
And when the little insanities
creep up from our throat, our teeth,
good soldiers holding their ground,
grind them down in our sleep. And praise
to the wolf with his sharp incisors,
the better to eat. And the ice-maiden's
teeth, sheathed in enamel, biting clean
through the bone. Oh we would never
depart from our eyeteeth, rooted dependably
above our unremarkable necks. And who
is not awed by the white buds of milkteeth
that sprout from red plushness and become
the cutting edge.

HEARING HIM TALK
Eric Heymann, 1903-1957

My own father died of swine flu, spent
his days reading Talmud in the back
room while my mother ran the store,
work-horse daughter of horse thieves.
That was my stock: one foot in heaven,
the other in mud. Never forgot that.

War already brewing when I first danced
with your mother in Karlsbad, she making
eyes at that dark Hungarian who looked
like Robert Taylor, American film star.
I know she didn't think much of me, though
for a stout man I dance a mean tango.

Followed her back to Prague with clear
intentions, ended up yelling at that
chicken-brained idiot who was her best
friend's brother, he believing Hitler
wouldn't invade: too well-off to be smart.
Hand-delivered twelve long-stemmed roses.

Had to drag your mother out. The others
perished. No matter how bad things are
they can always get worse. Stay liquid.
Avoid real estate, handsome men. Choose
one like a rock. Never cheat on taxes.
This country deserves every dime.

Sometimes I have no patience with lumps
in the horseradish sauce, you girls
for refusing to practice your scales.
I go up and down with the market.
You shouldn't take it so hard.
A lot of noise. The way I am.

THE MIRACLE OF BUBBLES

A woman drives to the video store
to rent a movie. It is Saturday night,
she is thinking of nothing in particular,
perhaps of how later she will pop popcorn
or hold hands with her husband and pretend
they are still in high school. On the way home a
plane drops from the sky, the wing shearing
the roof of her car, killing her instantly.
Here is a death, it could happen to any of us.
Her husband will struggle the rest of his days
to give shape to an event that does not mean
to be understood. Since memory cannot operate
without plot, he chooses the romantic—how young
she was, her lovely waist, or the ironic—if only
she had lost her keys, stopped for pizza.

At the precise moment the plane spiraled
out of control, he was lathering shampoo
into his daughter's hair, blonde and fine
as cornsilk, in love with his life, his
daughter, the earth (for "cornsilk" is how
he thought of her hair), in love with the miracle
of bubbles, how they rise in a slow dance,
swell and shimmer in the steamy air, then
dissolve as though they never were.

THE SUCCULENT EDGE

Everybody wants them in the woods, but nobody wants
them in the garden.
                      —John Mitchell, "White-tail Deer"

It is open season for stags
only. Hunters refuse to kill
antlerless deer, turning
this Connecticut hill town
into a whitetail kitchen:
stubs for fir, skeletons
for hemlock. A doe in rut
once trampled a woman
without provocation.

I have written a friend in Alaska,
Send wolves. I have written a friend
in Tanzania, Send lion's blood.
I have even collected clippings
from barbershops, stuffed them
into the toes of discarded pantyhose
and strung them along the trees
bordering my property. It was breached
that same night.

Now with a bound, one clears the wire
barrier between woodland and garden,
devouring begonias in search of sumac
and sassafras. So merciless
in her hunger, I suddenly think, Sister,
are we so very different, craving
as we do, surfeit for the belly,
buckskin for the back.

I KNOW WHY I AM HERE

I made one small hole in the breast
pocket of my husband's hunting jacket.
He loves this jacket, faded dull green
from early morning rain. I have done
my work neatly with his pocket-knife.
He will not be able to trace the incision
back to me. I have committed this act
because his arms are too short, his kisses
too dry and because he double-checks
doorknobs before departures.

I know why I am here, in the brass bed
of my lover. It is partly hunger, partly
love. I have brought strawberries
for the occasion. He buries them
one by one between my thighs, then sucks
them out whole, saying they taste of musk,
having ripened in darkness.

One day my husband will discover the damaged
pocket, and will ache with the loss of perfect
fabric. It is vital to add he is allergic
to dust and berries of all kinds, and thus
cannot partake of my legitimate fruit.

NIGHT WATCH

Give desire a shape, no matter
if that shape be squalor or sailor,
bronzed, blue-eyed, with muscles
of a man addicted to lifting weights.
You ache to touch his forearms.

Give him moves, subtle, deliberate,
and foreknowledge of where to put
his plate. Make it night. Have him
strip, swim the length of the turquoise
pool. Don't jump in. Listen instead

to the voluptuous rhythm of his wake.
When he emerges, naked, the water
dripping from his skin, it is you
who are exposed. Are you happier
for it, to know you could not bear

the tension of a slow seduction?
You choose this drama to unfold
as monologue, the way you will
replay this scene, your fierce
longing, and how you were taken.

THE GIFT

I

For his fortieth birthday a woman decides
to offer her husband a gift: he can tie her up
and have his way with her. If he gags her
with the terrycloth belt from his bathrobe,
she will be unable to protest. She goes
to the hardware store to buy rope, the kind
used to prevent boats from slipping away
from their moorings. All day she imagines
what her amenable husband will do—spank
her perhaps, but only playfully. What if
the game takes a more serious turn, if he
exults in his new-found power, beats her till
she's senseless or tickles her with a feather?
She consults with a friend over the phone.
Do it, the friend advises, he will be
your slave forever. The woman considers:
she has her eye on a new Persian carpet.
He could take her on it, his eyes rolling
with lust in their sockets. He'll pinch
her breasts, leave toothmarks on the exposed
skin of her neck. She will writhe her head
from side to side, try to call out "uncle"
through the thick wad of cloth stuffed in
her mouth. Imagining this she recalls her father
who spanked her bare rump when she was defiant,
and how pure she felt then, how justified.

II

A man comes home after a tedious day
at the office. His wife greets him
in a pink robe with babydoll sleeves.
"Happy Birthday," she says, handing him
a hank of rope. "Tie me up and have
your way with me." The man's spirits
revive, though he's peeved she has not
first prepared dinner. But he's a good
sport and busies himself at her ankles.
Hard work, this, he thinks. He's forgotten
everything he learned in the Boy Scouts.
Tying her wrists to the bedposts presents
more of a challenge. Soon he's grumbling:
he slaves all day, comes home to yet more
demands. After she is securely fastened,
he stands back to survey his handiwork.
He notes the mole on her ear, the muscular
thighs, the thin line of hair at her navel.
Then the phone rings and it is the hospital
saying his mother is in a coma. He dresses
hastily, grabs his car keys, departs. Hours
later he returns to his wife tangled up
in the bedroom. "The story of our lives,"
she snarls. "Your mother has always come first."
He heads for the kitchen, pops a chicken
pot pie in the microwave, most pleased and
astonished the knots he has tied still hold.

ALBANIAN VIRGIN

*If a girl of the Klementi tribe fiercely objected to the proposed
marriage, a blood feud could only be avoided by her swearing
an oath that she would never marry. Such a woman was called
an Albanian Virgin and ranked in the tribe as a man.*
—Carolyn Heilbrun, *Reinventing Womanhood*

i

The way he caught that horsefly
midair, the way he grinds his heel
into the dirt, taking pleasure
in the spider's slow death, the way
he throws a look at me as though
he already owns me—
I do not consent.

I shall smoke with the men.
I have seen them in the graying
light, their weapons close
to them always.

ii

The day is hot. My hair
is cropped. It is so still
I hear the bells clank
from the field. I swear the oath
before twelve witnesses
to forsake the intimate gestures
of all men, to remain chaste
as an unfreshened goat.

This night spent in solitude
on a rush mat, alone with the gravity
of my own body.

iii

I have learned to clip
the horns of goats, to slit
the throats of sheep
so the warm blood bathes
my fingers, and the animal feels
no pain, so sharp is my blade.

I am carried by dreams to the field
where I lie on the earth flanked by goats,
push a pale wet form from my loins.
It struggles to rise on its spindly legs.
I look deep into my goat-child's eyes.

iv

I eat with the men.
I chew charred slabs of meat
with the men. We smoke together,
my rough trousers chafing
the flesh of my thighs.

I gaze at the women who sit
in tight circles, pounding
pestles into stone bowls.

My lungs fill
with harsh comforting smoke.

UNINVITED GUESTS

Three can keep a secret if two are corpses.
—Yiddish folk saying

Even the dead can't keep
a secret. They barge in,
sit at your table, demanding
to be served. They bang
their spoons like children
crying, *Feed me! Feed me!*
And you have never prepared
enough.

   Once you would have welcomed
the dead, begged Mother to set out
extra plates. But now they consume
what was promised to the living.
They climb into the marriage bed
with their own unearthly linen,
whispering old secrets you wish
they would keep to themselves.

WHAT I DWELL ON

We never come to thoughts. They come to us.
—Martin Heidegger

It has been months since a good
night's sleep, that landing you come
to at the foot of the stairs. Instead,
two-hour catnaps before springing
awake as though what is required of me
is vigilance. I cannot tell you
what I think walking the long corridor
to the kitchen for a sip of juice, or
wandering into my son's room to examine
his face, the radical purity of something
not quite formed. At night the face becomes
more like itself, bones make their minor
shifts and settle, like a house sinking
as it contracts, the pliant earth
rising up to receive it, even the windows,
the vanishing roof. When a man jumps
from a great height he dies of suffocation,
not impact. I fear those twin perils, and
falling, now falling asleep. Miser or thief,
I hold to what I know. No one sneaks up
from behind, pushes me over the balustrade.
And no one would claim me, breathless
and shattered from the depths of sleep.

NÉE MAGGIE MALONE

She didn't shave her legs or underarms
because her husband said it was unnatural
which is fine in Zagreb but in summer
heat at the Safeway she felt savage
like when she'd had to go in the middle of
the night at his family's farmhouse and relieved
herself in a pot which she hid in the closet.

That summer the pick-up died while he was restoring
houses on Capitol Hill for "that bastard Grodski
doesn't he know I'm craftsman   no bubbles when I
paint walls" and that summer Rudy still suckled at
Maggie's breast though he was four and her female
friends thought it bizarre even perverse.

What would they say if they knew he crawled nightly
into their bed wetting the sheets   Maggie
stumbling for the child's cot while father and son
slept on together.

Then he was fired by that bastard Grodski who said
he was arrogant and Maggie told friends he quit
because he couldn't take orders from a crook
who didn't appreciate fine work.

They were poorer next summer and he said "Save money
make sheets" and she thought about it   then he said
"Be useful   learn Croatian" and he gave her a dictionary
and she tried in late afternoons to say the sounds
while the new baby nursed and Rudy clung monkey-like
to her furry legs.

Irish jigs played on the phonograph   she thought
I should make sheets   I should learn Croatian
She hummed the reels thinking   I'd like to
shuffle stomp stomp stomp shuffle stomp stomp stomp

QUESTION OF AESTHETICS

He never wrote a letter without
the words "despair" or "terror"
as in, "Even as a child I knew
despair," or, "How to turn
this terror into art." How romantic
it seemed then, like living
a Russian novel. His final note
read, "Tell her our relationship
was fully satisfying in every way."

No one ever says how thrilling
pain is, how it takes you like
a lover, how your body cringes
before surrender. At first
you cry no, no, then swoon
into its burly arms. You should see
your open mouth, your breath coming
in harsh gasps. Trust pain to find
the choicest part, the marrow,
and suck out resolve, leaving you
limp. But oh, how you'll sleep.

The only burden heavier than pain
is boredom, want of danger. When I
teach *Anna Karenina* to young girls,
I say, "Every woman should experience
one disastrous love affair and survive."
How like a woman Anna was, to hesitate
because she could not bear to throw
her red purse away. How like a man
he was to put a bullet someplace deadly.
As a woman who's survived, I see boredom
now as comfort, devotion as something
precious, and death in any form,
a slap across the face.

SONG WHILE ARRANGING JASMINE
AND JEWELWEED

1

You ask me, when did it begin?
When I saw you at the Mercado
sniffing a cantaloupe. Ramon!
The way you held that melon it must
have ripened in your hand. That night
in the ballroom, it was your sparkling
moustache, the pearl stud in your tie.
And when you entered me it was as though
you already knew me, so sure was your beat,
so emphatic my reply. Adorado! I told you
I had many lovers. You knew I lied.

2

When you give me that cock-
eyed, cross-eyed, pie-eyed
look, oh my pet I know
you're feeling the itch
to travel. That's when
I stick a rose in my hair,
light a cigarillo and offer
to button your spanking white
shirt. Adios, Ramon, bye bye!
I shut the door with finesse
and greet my own heart, sweet
heart, faithful dumb pumper.

3

Take care where you plant your feet,
my Latin-American strongman.
There's a hot tarantella on the tip
of my tongue. Don't tell me to shut
my mouth. I say what I please.
And if there's an earthquake, I get
the doorway. So there's a dead one
floating in the milk. A cockroach here
can be rocked in a cradle. I don't
wear these pointy shoes for nothing.
I am no dumb blonde you swept away.
I play my part with proper agitation.

4

It's Sunday, and here comes Ramon.
All is forgiven, my docile lambkin!
Let's bleat together under the covers.
Come nuzzle the pale globe of my belly,
Come drink from my goblet of love.

SUBTITLES

There was always something forbidden
about foreign films, as though reading
subtitles afforded a glimpse into
the still untranslated adult world.
I had to board a bus, then walk up

Lefferts Boulevard, past outdoor fish
stalls and enormous-breasted women
guarding fruit. In this flourishing
neighborhood was *The Circle*, the one
theatre in Queens that featured

foreign films. It was here I saw
Kurasawa's *Yojimbo*, warrior gone amuck
with exquisite swordplay. A human wrist
carried off by a dog while the town
smolders, the wreckage so complete

nothing is left whole. This is the end
result of formal perfection—Samurai
turned mercenary; an old man trussed-up,
suspended from a tree, knowing he's safer
where he is. So when the man next to me

places his hand on my thigh, I sit in my
plush seat and say nothing. On screen
the hero drinks hot blood. Already he
is outdated. And in the dark, a touch
light and hesitant, perhaps imagined.

NIGHT AT THE OPERA

Although Aida and Rhadames are buried alive
in a crypt, they sing a long and complicated
duet which requires much breath. I want
to cry out, "Save air!" because I am eight
and living long is of great concern to me
and I don't understand that kind of love.
Only synagogue bores me more than opera
and for a similar reason: nothing makes sense.
During the High Holy Days, guttural sounds
engulf me, and there is all this standing up
and sitting down. The congregants seem
more intrigued by each other than with God.
One commandment says not to covet. I don't
know what that means, but I love the word.
It reminds me of my favorite blanket, its
much-nuzzled satin binding. I've been told
to give it up, but I can't, nor my thumb, most
faithful companion. My feet throb, cramped
in black Maryjanes. On stage, the lovers
swoon into each other's arms and die, while
overhead, hymns and sacred dance continue
without my participation or consent.

WHAT WE SHALL BECOME

From these heights the war
blazes in primary colors, banners
magnificent. From here the scale

of human suffering is inconsequential.
Down there, under the hooves, clumps
of dirt churn and fly, bodies fall.

What alters if the gods pity or mock us?
Once there was a great Lord who sired three
sons—one foolish, one bloodthirsty,

one noble and true. They turn on each other
like wild dogs. When reconciliation seems
almost impossible, a musket misfires, picks off

the noble son. He drops to the ground,
stone dead. His father learns the meaning
of random universe, clutches his throat

and chokes. This story repeats itself
generation after generation. Our hearts
will always go out to a man on the brink

of lunacy, since we seem to fear losing
our wits even more than our lives. Is there
salt in the castle strongroom? There is

always salt. Salt for the preservation
of meat, a rival's severed head, to remind us
of what we once were, what we have replaced.

FIRST THERE WAS LIGHT AND THAT
BEGINS THE NARRATIVE

Earthly Fare

Lizard, foxglove, piglet, Adam
busies himself in the Garden
naming, syllables spilling
out of his mouth so that even
while steeped in contemplation,
wildebeest, redbud, he cannot stop.
He babbles, delights in the pitch
of his voice, until exhausted
he falls into slumber, awakens
to Woman, fully formed. God knows
he needs conversation, but she's
had no childhood to speak of
and hers is a world already
defined. Under munificent leaves
of the fig tree and under the vast
dome of sky, Adam's stuttering fingers
explore her. She's asking questions
like who and wherefore and why and just
because He says so? and reaches out
for what pleases her eye. It tastes
good and she doesn't die. Her baby
Abel, wet-breath, not lasting, he
shows her how. No one prepared
her, no mother with sweetcakes
who crooned lullabies, no mother at all,
just no and you can't, without
explanation. So like a father not
to embellish, no margin for error, no
one more chance. He had no mother either,
no honey with the bitter pill, no push
and pull, only a stunning shock of light.

After Eden
If she had known the gestures
of reproach, dark scowls, the stony
back, lingered, she'd have prayed
harder for a little girl, named her
something silly and inconsequential,
like Fleur or Belle, not burdened her
with the task of making it right
between them. But as it was, Cain,
acquisition, was meant to buy back
Adam's love. So there were strings.
Small wonder he grew sharp—
featured as a rodent, sniffed the air
to test if it was safe to breathe. She couldn't
bear the look of him. And close
as breath was memory of
drought, the year thistle and
sting-bush flourished,
and sustenance, a thin gruel of tuber
and barley. Eve, heavy again
with child, turned inward, left
Cain to wander after his father in
the pock-marked clay.
Then Eve, flanked by starving cows,
crouched in the parched field and
then the wet slippery child sliding
out, strands of fine black hair tracing
its skull, and the cows
rearranging their loosened flesh
as Eve held
the child to her breast. "Wet breath,"
she called him, because his birth
augured rain. And when it came,
the earth unfolded, a paradise of green.

Granted One
At first she thought God loved
her most, to have dealt her such
affliction. It proved she was
His special girl. Not that Adam
didn't care, just more accustomed
to the vagaries of the weather, wind
and rain and never the same day
twice. Then too, he was so grateful
Cain survived, he became almost tender,
too late to halt Eve's descent
into an absence of recall. She wandered
the fields, stripping the husks off
sheaves of corn, and making dolls
for "little Fleur." She whispered
incessantly to her and sang strange
rhyming songs. When Adam tried
to bring her back, she accused him
of intruding. The dolls crowded
their bed at night and sat with them
at supper. And thus time passed.
Eve's hair turned brittle, then grey,
so that once when she caught sight
of herself, she greeted that woman
with polite reserve. One spring, mist
shrouding the meadows like baby's breath,
Adam came to her with all the need
and urgency of a young man. The tilt
of his head, his shyly offered bouquet
of blossoms, reminded her of Abel
and Eve lay down and took him in.
afterwards, she wept. Another son
was born, Shet, Granted One.

BALANCING ACT

Up here on the high wire it's a sheer sure-
footed dance, a one-night mission
under the Big Top, without a safety net

to cushion. It's the taunting misstep, the
sharp intake of breath, exhalations
of the squeamish egging me on, and the world

marble-smooth, veined to the core, perched
on the tip of my tongue. I juggle spangled
orbs from one palm to another, a marriage

of holding on and letting go. You'd think by
now I'd let it fall, the world cracked open
like a skull, bits of hair, feathers,

the loose associations. But once I knew the
buttons on a fly, the upturned collar, the
child licking her fingers imagining

an Africa, I knew all matter while compressed is
no longer solitary. Ask me how I keep it twirling,
defying gravity with every turn—

I'll never tell. You won't read fear in
eyes that glitter, dazzle, take you
by storm. Come one, come all, observe

communion with infinity. See the fabulous
steps, the foolhardy toes. Be amazed
by the pupil of possibility.

DEFINITIVE ACT

A magician saws a woman in half
by accident, says, "I guess I need

more practice." He climbs inside
his coffer of mirrors to perfect

his craft. Any fracture increases
the chance for dialogue: "Lady,"

he says, "illusion makes the body
radiant, makes it bleed." Reader,

you are the errant half I am
longing for, longing to cleave.

                    *

What a mess she's left, the lamp
still burning, scattered hairpins,
her spare tutu. She'd insisted

on small amenities, this lamp
for example, its Tiffany shade.
Light wasn't the issue, she wanted

things pretty, an intimacy beyond
performance, beyond applause.
She wanted post-mortems, to wear

her tuxedo, his top hat, to ruffle
her doves. He wanted to shut her
up, confine her to quarters. Then

down on his knees, like a beggar,
a dog, down on all fours, tongue
at the keyhole, tongue like a key.

*

This isn't a fable, here
is the coffer, the keyhole,
the mirror that saves you
from torpor, from me.

ELEMENTAL COSMOLOGY

The rooster crows with his eyes shut because he crows from memory.
—Yiddish folk saying

A rooster once crowed with his eyes
open because he wanted to see
the morning unfold. So smitten
was he by the first tinge
of dawn, he stopped singing.
Then the sun ceased her ascent,
feet froze on their way
out of bed, mouths stiffened
into yawns. What will release

this landscape to its usual
bustle, and the hovering soul
waiting to be born, to take on
its shadow? Everything rests

on the rooster's desire
for the sun, old sweetheart.
He must close his eyes to resume
his passionate crowing.

BORDER DISPATCH

In a remote district an old man
consoles himself with pornographic
photos, enraptured by animal acts
he no longer performs. Just as

the acne-scarred motorcycle mechanic
slicks his eye over the road and takes
time with tools. Precision is slow work,

a young girl picking a scab off her knee
but sparing the layer of pale pink skin.
This is what happens when rollerskates

travel faster than the body lagging
behind like a spent bloodhound
who fails to keep pace with the fox.

*

A woman fastening her dress
studies the form
sprawled on the bed.
Men come, she thinks,
to sleep, to abandon
themselves to sleep.
The young ones
curl up like puppies
protecting their soft parts.
She inspects the contents
of his wallet, removes
a tenspot, applies
fresh lipstick in the dark.

*

The early light of morning is
impartial, leaf rot, the black
ribs of trees as indistinct as
the moral nature of the world,
the way we graduate from symbol
to the infinitesimal. Now
we are nameless, now without
income. Somewhere a window
opens and an arm extends, palm
up as if in supplication. What
will fall from the sky today?

THE FUTURE HAS ALREADY HAPPENED

Imagine I'm Little Red Riding Hood
and you're the woodcutter and you've
read it too. Imagine the wild Caesarean,
the ax and its fresh cut, the blade
running deep. And me springing out
to dance on the planked floor with Granny
in her white nightdress, soft and white
to the touch. Oh the body and its sweet
decay! But I leap ahead of the story.
Years later we meet and we marry, then
there's the birthing and the baking of
cookies to be carried in a basket
by the girl setting off in her red hood.

from

Marvelous Pursuits

(1995)

IT NEEDS BRAINS

Maupassant, prodigious lover, swore
he could come twenty times in a row
and never tire. He took a dancer
from the Folies Bergère six times
in an hour (there was a bookkeeper
who counted) then strode across the hall
and came thrice more with a prostitute.
He valued carnal success above his art:
"It needs brains to give another pleasure."

Same Maupassant fell for Gisèle d'Estoc,
her close-cropped hair, her manly attire.
She hankered for a trapeze artiste
from le Cirque Medrane, then stabbed her
in the thigh. Gisèle shared with Guy
her slimhipped women, hashish, ether.

But the only woman he ever loved was
"L'Inconnue." She haunted his imagination:
"intensely sensuous, self-controlled,
soulful, yet a coquette." What woman wouldn't cry,
"C'est moi!" relieved to be recognized.

Oh, Guy, come feast on me, my ambiguities
are singular. Austerity and razzledazzle.
Don't be seduced by the sheer extravagance
of numbers. You called pursuit of *The Unknown*
life's grand adventure. There is no other.

BALLAD OF THE ID

I am your rose hips and bunting and bootleg
and I am your black bangs those devil's
spikes and I am your spine when you lie
down in ticklegrass the zipper the cock
all glistening and white and I am the stars
that roll in their sockets that blink on
the night I could be Gibraltar or jukebox
or drumstick without me you're puny and
pallid and prudish and with you are banquet
a wishbone with tassles that time in the bistro
I bit your sister and squealed on the porter
and who pulled you out of the muck of intention
who sang hosannas for spunk and risk who shorted
the sheets who stole your tom-tom
just ask and I'll you I did I did

TECTONICS

Once I have committed
your body to memory, I can begin
to go beneath the surface of skin,
follicle, pore. The orphaned mother
who birthed you now is mine,
that scrappy boy at loggerheads
with the world, I claim him,
and as for you, you absorb
the brunt of my father's rage.
This is what is meant to cleave,
to take on sorrows we do not own
and make them ours, so intimate
a coupling. And that is why
in love's afterglow I feel close
to tears—something has been split
open, and if the body is like
the earth's crust, the deeper
the fault, the more it can hold.

CRAZY JANE'S RETURN

Crazy Jane.   Love, when after love we lie
our booty spent, still
your languid fingers toy
at sites of merriment
and still you tarry by my side
though your rod be bent.

You used to scuttle from my bed
at first cock's crow, but now
you linger, yawn instead
and do not go, you do not go
as if you're paying homage to
love's work in field and furrow.

Wild Jack.   I know we both shall rise again
in no mean hour's time
to squeal as do our barnyard kin
(though some deem it a crime)
at holy trough and sacred sty
where the soul roots, sublime.

Many former loves I've known,
many with biblical names,
but none could heal or satisfy
like my Crazy Jane, and none
was more wholly sane.
There was none more holy sane.

Crazy Jane.   Oh crimson is your tongue, your speech,
what would the Bishop say?
Never Heaven shall you reach!
where the likes of him do bray.
But Heaven have we found on earth,
down on all fours we pray.

A MATTER OF CHOICE

"Pet or meat?" the braless
woman asks. Under each arm
she cradles a rabbit. This

is a woman who knows how
to kill: "Just lay them
on the ground and lop off

their heads." And how
to give pleasure—her two
thumbs press a vein in each

rabbit's neck. Love,
sometimes when you enter
I bare my teeth. Salt

or sweet? The body decides
since the body must answer
to curious, various hungers.

SUPEREGO SERENADE

Call me vicious rigid but each and every
moment I'm besieged by want and want and want
you greedy child your plump fist in your mouth
if not for me you'd eat a tree house gulp
down the very world itself and I know even if
you don't that inside every fat woman is
a fatter one so bless me now and keep your foul
tongue furled inside your mouth I'm here to teach
control to take control and if I sometimes squat
to hold you down I'm no pansy I can take your
rage and dish it out you pig you cow you two bit
whore of Babylon who'd take a crack at every
hunk who's got two balls inside his pants it's up
to me to ladle guilt and blame and don't and don't
to chill you with an image of your mother who's realer
than your mother though she'll be blowzy cheap
and flicking ashes on your cheek you'll know
she's out to kill you with that dagger tucked
inside her stockinged thigh her smartly crayoned
eyebrows cut a jagged pathway to her temple so
reap your just desserts for lusting after taken
men for boys for old old men and as an encore
I'll send in my hit squad to gun you down and for
the mop-up job here comes the crocodile with snapping
jaws you'll wake up with the sweats but fess up
you're relieved to count on me sure as shootin'

FORESHADOWS

Now that I've read
the first draft of your body
I can already tell
the rough places
where there is need
for further exploration.
In due time the clenched
jaws will release a flurry
of words, unearthing
the grave heart
from its vault of ribs.
And since there already is
perfection, the soft mounds
of your fingers, the exquisite
way they interpret my spine,
well then, I can wait
for the rest, the story
your tongue will tell
to the flesh and its slow unfolding.

HEROICS

Love calls for a great act
of the imagination. We haul
ourselves out of the brackish past
and again it's by touch
that we know it. Awash

in rapture the human heart
cries for expression, as Aida
and Rhadames hasten by singing
their own demise. Love, our story
has all the ingredients

of high drama—the night sky
ablaze with scuds and you
trapped in a sealed room,
tachycardia. Meanwhile, I drive
my wasted mother to hospitals

which refuse to admit her.
Events conspire. Impossible
to discount the bodies we're heir to.
The day before my mother's lover died
he seized her hair and tried to mount her

from behind. Your father
at eighty-four stripped himself naked
and made obscene gestures.
A ludicrous passion survives. Nobody
tells us this. No consoling arias.

IN YOUR ABSENCE

At first it was your body
I missed, its trappings. This
has not changed. I still feel less
composed without you. But the weight
of your presence I do not miss. Nor
your shambling through my house.
I do not. Miss it, I mean. And here

we thought inertia was the way
of things. How lethargy has
its own momentum. The world is ripe
with calamity. I have never
slept better. Where you are—
the holy land, the hotbed
of disputed claims. Sharing quarters

with your wife. Debilitating meals
at the kitchen table where your heartburn
vanishes. "We're used to it," you say
of war, as though it were weather,
could be sealed out. Even
the keyhole. What we had. I mean
we slept through it all, the fall

and its implications. How spacious
absence is. Restorative. Elsewhere, and long ago,
mammoths neared the land bridge, lifted
one lumbering foot after another,
sustained by arctic ice.

WAR DOESN'T WANT

War doesn't want to be
an arcade game, doesn't
want an enemy a blip
on the radar screen.
It doesn't want a victor
with the best eye-hand
coordination. It wants
the thrill of killing
at intimate range, wants
the torch, the stench
of singed flesh (the skin
tastes best). It hates
dining alone, making death
with strangers. It wants
to know what it's eating.

A SMALL MATTER

To see clearly, first
one must make things complicated.
Which is why the Chinese delight
in labyrinths. And why
they fill their homes
with many children. Only demons
walk a straight path. And I
who lived in solitude so long
it fits me like a slipper. It's not
your barbs that turn me wild,
it's your cursed meddling, reminding me
that you've unpacked. Only God
sees what's behind that nude
reclining on the grass. Perhaps
the one who used the brush.
Small wonder, then, this rage
for order. A lie, but simple.

HUNDESLEBEN

I

Red ones. White ones. Yellow
and green ones. My mother lives
from pill to pill, a pill
for every occasion. For pain.
Sleep. Swelling. Nerves.
For blood. Bowels. *Hundesleben*,
she says. A dog's life. Years ago
it was Chuckles, sweet jellies
at the movies. She wouldn't eat
the green ones. Chuckles. Now
pills. We all know of the black
purse she keeps by her pillow,
her stash. And let her. Even though
they make her wet, cry out in Czech
for her second dead husband. Swaddle
her in pampers, and let her. Once
we counted forty blue pills clustered
on her sheets. Forty. For sorrow.
Forget-me-nots. Toxic bouquet.

II

During our time apart, I committed
unnatural acts: soaped my mother's
bald pubis, shoved her rectum back
into the cavity so near the one
that birthed me. She cursed me
in Czech, called me a lowdown cur
when I denied her Halcion. Seeing you stoop
to lift your battered vinyl suitcase,
no one would have faulted me had I chosen
to ship you back. Not you. Especially
you who would have said the fates delight
in sport. As it was, a pure gladness
rose up in me, and it mattered not at all
that you were not rich, not young, not
savvy. I wanted to take you in, and
be taken. They say it is always
the wrong person. You are not
the wrong person. You are not my mother
though you bring me your failed flesh.
You are not my father whose severity,
he thought, would train me for life. No,
you are a simple man whose first allegiance
is to the parched land of origin turning
evergreen and succulent from *hundesleben*,
this worrying and burying familiar bones.

MARVELOUS PURSUITS

Overture
A man with two mistresses desires
nothing but peace and tranquility.
He suffers if they should quarrel,
preferring their foreheads unwrinkled.

One day he receives a letter.
The words leap out in bold
typeface: "Cuckold. Cuckold.
More to follow. A neighbor."

He cannot imagine who sent it.
He is obsessed with curiosity.
Which neighbor? Which mistress?
Both mistresses occupy luxury flats.

Both mistresses occupy luxury flats.
Rosa's furnished in bone-white and black
and Blanca's in all shades of rose.

Rosa and Blanca, like two sisters,
one naughty and hot, quick to anger,
the other so plump and luxuriant.

On her rose settee sits Blanca,
her fingers caressing the keys
of the old Royal typewriter salvaged
from her dear late father's estate.

On her rose settee sits Blanca,
puffing slowly on a cigarillo.
Soon she will put on her poncho,
take an afternoon stroll to the maildrop.

Wanton Modulations

The hydrangea, having never been
so purple as this particular year,
cast purple shadows on the cobbled
walk which leads to the front porch
of the house on Pompano Street where
Marta rocks in rhythmic frenzy on slats
that slope and creak from dry rot.

This morning as her husband donned
his starched white shirt, she noted
purple bruises on his shoulder blades
like dark cherries, a message, perhaps,
from either one of his two mistresses,
intended, surely, for her eyes alone.

Jealous? No. She knows to him she is
the one who darns his black silk socks,
takes too lax a hand with kitchen maids
who fail to dust the parlor to perfection.
Let him dwell on youthful breasts, sweet
abundant flesh of those who hold him gaily.

Daily, she bids her spouse a gray farewell,
retires to the rocker, her faded housedress
a once-wild floral print. In undergarments
clean and frilly, she awaits the piano tuner
who comes faithfully at noon when cobbles
on the walkway are their own color.

Leitmotif

The piano tuner never comes empty
handed. Today he brings a tiny tart
of marzipan and raspberries. Perched
sedately on white wicker, he observes
formalities, inquires of the kitchen
maids, their foolish superstitions. Marta
tells in tremulous trill of the wounded
bird who found its way into the larder,
how she herself released it. The piano,
he asks, how has it been behaving?
He plays a slow arpeggio, cocks
an ear for off-key tones. He has
his way with strings, tunes them taut
or slack until each note rings out
according to its true pitch.

Seasonal Variation

The piano tuner's mother foretells
the weather. Like a bullfrog,
her arthritic hip senses rain.
Nothing to be done but make a trip
to the doctor who packs her in
medicinal mud imported from Ischia.

Alas, it has come to this: athletic
limbs that danced tarantellas until
daybreak, paddle about in support hose.
Of late she's taken to her rosary, and
a small nip of sherry before vespers.
Her angelic son, runt of the litter,
plays Scarlatti after sunset, balding
pate glowing like an unhatched egg.

Inverted Turn
With cold-blooded haste, he breaks off
contact with his two mistresses, takes
a chamois cloth and polishes his ox-blood
wingtips, revealing the tiny pin-pricks
like pores on the nose of the shoe, visible
as the blue tattoo of a songbird – a thrush –
on his chest, Marta Forever indelible,
inscribed just yesterday on his willing flesh.

Overcome by fever, he must take
to bed, advised by doctors to abstain
from physical exertion which might lower
his body's resistance to fight the strain
of infection. Marta shuffles in slippers,
brings fruit juice, wraps a cool compress
on his wound. If she feels desperate,
trapped, she does not show it, nor regret
for her affair, exposed, thus ruined.

His wife, so recently reviled and scorned
by him for newer, more exotic flesh,
becomes by infidelity transformed
into the forbidden erotic, object
of his single-minded lust. Her ample
girth once filled him with disgust, the sheer
expanse of it, but viewed in betrayal's
light, is suddenly, irresistibly dear.

Perfect Interval
Rosa, supine, takes the last
rays of sun, the last drops
of oil, Blanca's insistent

palm lifting flesh from bone.
Muscles contract in the cave
of the groin as Rosa turns,

spring lamb on a spit, feels
a quicksilver tongue moisten
her lips. She is used to being

adored, the momentary shadow
her lids absorb, that grip. She
answers with hips, thighs, clenched

toes, finding in a state of tension,
repose. A circular brick wall
permits this feline world of curve

and claw where orchids bloom
multitudinous as weeds, concealed
from marauders, their scorched eyes.

Capitulation
And wouldn't we always always slip
into the hot slick coat of it,
spurning food to feel our mouths
go dry with it, stretch out
our arms for this one's lust,
that one's need? We tremble
into being, take in the morning's
striking palette, our lips dusted

with the taste of it. Those sounds
we make, wouldn't they be torn out
by the root, and the wounds
suffered gladly? Anima, animus, we
descend into our evolutionary niche, wild,
demonic, from the bliss of it.

FUN WITH DICK

If to be in life is to make
choices, I'm in it. So says
my private eye whom I'll call
Dick. Dick and I hold this
rendezvous under potted palms
in a posh hotel. It seems
I've chosen this dime-store novel
plot to play in. Dick states
my best shot: he tracks my husband
to Lulu Labelle who believes
in knots. Or some sweet thing
who's under twenty. Or a guy.
Something he wouldn't want
to get around. And then,
says Dick, you swap.
Mexican standoff.
          You know, yawns Dick,
slouched in a barrel chair, your hubby
called me. To follow you. Such
a big world, I think, and only
one Dick. I trust Dick, more
than lawyers or lovers. I trust
his stale clichés, their sudden ring
of truth, like koans—*fight fire*
with fire. It all comes down
to dollars and cents. I'm in
a fix, I say. No, says Dick,
you're in life. Tonight he'll go
hear Milli Vanilli, teeny bop
rockers. Ensconced between the wife
and daughter, he'll plug his ears
with cotton, whistle Cole Porter
under his breath, a beatific
smile flirting on his lips.

GIRL TRADES BABY FOR PROM DRESS
—National Enquirer

How smug we feel, we who measure want
in dollops, but imagine her, wanting
to distraction and to be so trapped.
That's how much she wants the blue
chiffon with blue spaghetti straps,
blue rose pinned to the waist and shoes
dyed to match. She wants the gardenia
wristlet, to dance under the bluest moon,
a chance to be elected queen, to neck
in a rented limousine. A horse
isn't hers to give, nor gold,
nor tea. Kings have traded more,
been called heroic. When Anna
abandoned Sergei, wasn't she tragic?
These days I feel my own parched
throat, the bedrock crumbling.
For the fecundity of your embrace
I too would pay, and dearly.

UNDERSTUDY

After her second husband died
I thought my mother would
at last define herself, stop
the hard work of being adored.
I was wrong. Within a year there
was another man, colder,
harder, like the diamonds
he used to cut in Bruges. Now
he's 94, reduced to outline,
using the jeweller's loupe
to decipher the headlines.
Arthritis has altered my mother's
smile to grimace. To see them
holding hands, their heads
slumped forward as they doze,
is to see two shadow selves
barely tethered to earth.

To move forward into your own
life, first, they say, you must
resolve anger. Meaning, I thought,
to forgive. Some things cannot
be forgiven—Mother banishing me
from Father's deathbed, Father
striking out when I was little.
I only played a bit part
in their dramas. What was I
rehearsing for? For this,
to help my mother hobble
from bed to vanity
where cosmetic jars still line
the counter? She will not,
I know, reach for the magnifying
mirror where once she checked
her expression. With me
beside her, she never could
bear the sight of herself.

THERE FOR THE GRACE

There for the grace of god there
for the grace there for the window
the housekeeper carelessly left
ajar for the five-year-old boy
who fell from the fifty-third
floor there for the musician his
father and his guitar there for
the mother the mother and there
for the cruise ship out for a cruise
for the cripple whose wheelchair
was pushed and tumbled down into
the Mediterranean there for the blue
of the sea of the starling and finch
and the hyacinth there for the lover
who follows the script who touches
the lips and within the mystère
there for the sweet inhalation of breath
for the arm casually raised to brush
back the hair there for the grace
of god for the grace of earth we go

THEIR SPOUSES COULD PLAY

Their spouses could play canasta at the cemetery
is how the joke went the summer four members
of the refugee circle died. One of the players

would be my mother, chic in her widow's weeds,
slapping the red threes down. And how the dead
would kibitz, tally the pebbles the living left

to mark their visits. Herr Glauber came courting
before the first frost. The night of his wife's
burial, the phone rang and my mother and I answered

at once. I heard them discussing blueprints and the bidet
for the new master bathroom, and that I must be sent to live
with his pregnant daughter. And so it came to pass—

my senior year at the house on Juno Street, witness
to my stepsister's swelling belly, and I was not
unhappy there, the small seed of grief tucked

in my gullet. It flourished over the years
and I tend it even now, as my mother lies dying
in the remodeled bedroom painted dark teal, scenes

of the tropics splashed on the walls. I have never
spoken of this, the exile from the house my father
built, my mother drugged on a rented hospital bed

and the vines that grip my cold and capable heart.

ALARUMS AND EXCURSIONS

Distressed and distraught over a broken heart
a woman decides she needs protection. Enter
Francis Drake from Be Secure. What I'm selling
he says, is peace of mind. The system he touts
is used by the Navy and NASA alike. Something
like killing a fly with a bulldozer, she says,
since she's mainly concerned about her back
door. Like his namesake, Drake's been around,
has even defeated armadas, pirates greedy
for foreign gold. He calmly recites drastic
scenarios—taken hostage while carting groceries,
stun-gun for the dog, the fire that travels
90 feet-per-second. Or, he says, you could
fall downstairs and break both legs. How
do I know, she asks, you're not a serial killer
or a scam artist? Adele, he says (her given
name), you don't. She notes his fingernails
trimmed and clean, and his eyes a benevolent
baby blue. The power surge, he adds, is a sweet
touch, as she imagines his and how it would feel
to be hitched to a man who knows the tricks of breaking
and entering and how to secure all she holds
dear from those who would trespass against her.

TALE FROM THE NORTHWOODS
Charles Van Riper, pioneer in the field of stuttering

Once by drowning, once by hanging, once
by inhaling carbon monoxide, three
attempts before I was thirty, all

failures. All because of a tangled
tongue. And a father who beat me
for the filthy habit, calling it akin

to masturbation. The summer I pretended
to be deaf and dumb. The quack cures,
cruel experiments, needles in the mouth,

psychotropic drugs. Singing. The ordeal
of going to the corner store for Dill's
pipe cleaner. Of walking out without.

Aspirations zero, until I hitched a ride
with a farmer who said don't labor so hard,
just stutter better, let the syllables

leak out. I might have been St. Paul
on the road to Damascus. Soon a man
appeared in spotless attire making odious

sounds. Took him to a calving. Up
to his shoulder in the bloody muck.
Made him extract the afterbirth, dump it

in a bucket. The man turned sloppier,
the stutter, cleaner. Every case
a metaphor to deconstruct, unleashing

the unsayable, the choked back flood.

WHAT IS SERVED

There must be an appetite for grief.
How else explain this gnawing on memory
until its bones are clean? The soul
barks and barks for its ration
of remembered things—the smell
of tangerines, undergarments stripped
like husks, exposing flesh as willful
and imperative. And how surrender
nourishes deliverance.
                         Now we are
swollen with absence and abstinence
tucks in our sheets. In our mouths
the aftertaste of satiety. Narrow
the bed we lie in, ample, our need.

STORMY PETREL
for Cully Gage

Before she must leave for the long
flight East, the old man insists
they descend the cellar steps, past
hand-hewn beams, past the massive
tree trunk he calls Atlas. Here
in the wine and fruit room, ten years
after his wife's death, are mason jars
filled with her pickles and peaches.
Beyond, in a closet, rests the skull
of an Indian girl. He calls her *Nokomis*
and tells how she died from a blow
to the right ear. He shows the woman
the hole. He discovered the skull
in the tangled roots of an upended oak.
No other bones. Wolves carried them off
says the man, no stranger to woods or habits
of wolves. But the skull wouldn't fit
in their great jaws so he took it home
to this dark cellar in Kalamazoo, childhood
name for nowhere. And places it now
in the woman's palm. She runs her fingertips
over the burnished bone. It is not cold.

*

I've been thinking, he said, only
a few hours later, during a meal
of venison sausage and warmed-over
pasty, a loggerman's breakfast, what
kind of bird you are (for you are
a bird) and I've finally come up
with the answer: stormy petrel. You dive

again and again into the salty
waves but always emerge triumphant.
The old man smiles, satisfied.
The woman asks if she should change
her feathers. He laughs and says
she couldn't even if she wanted to
and why would she want to.

*

Arriving home, she heads straight
for the Audubon, learns her habitat

is the open sea. Her diet consists
of small shrimp and plankton. She seldom

follows boats. She is jet black,
has a white rump, forked tail, erratic

flight. She resorts to rocky islands
to breed under cover of darkness, filling

the air with nocturnal trills. She lays
one white egg. When ruffled she emits

a musky odor. And this: she contains
so much oil that even after death

if a wick is lit in her throat
it will burn for months. There are times

she has yearned for an ordinary life,
hearth, husband, balanced meals prepared

on schedule. Rues the day she was born
to perpetual flight, and the burning.

from

The Royal Baker's Daughter

(2008)

ALUMINUM

My father loved whatever was new—like the aluminum
pan he brought home one night, dangling it by its ring
from his pinky. "Look how light it is!" he crowed,
glancing with scorn at the cast iron skillet. He never
stepped into the kitchen, yet there he was, in a merry mood
frying up bacon. My sister and I were enchanted, perched

on red leatherette chairs swinging our legs. Soon the strips
pale and pink as the skin under a scab were trembling
in a pool of grease. Then my father swirled the pan so
the bacon wouldn't stick, spilling fat onto the burner, that's
how light it was, the pan. Flames shot up to the ceiling.

It stayed black until the painters came. I don't remember
who cleaned up the mess, only that he didn't lose
his temper—at me for being a chatterbox, or my sister
for chewing her braids. And he didn't hit us, either. Even
he couldn't blame the pan, only the hand that held it.

CARVEL

In the summer, when the days were light longer,
we'd pile in the car and drive down Metropolitan
Avenue for soft ice cream at Carvel's. Those nights
we could have been a regular American family out
for a spin, whose father maybe tossed a ball
with his kids, or tousled their hair, or let himself
be tickled. But we knew his moods would return,
when we'd tiptoe around the house, lay low. This
was the fifties, there was Korea, but it was far away
and it wasn't our war and they weren't murdering
our people. Later I'd learn, but only much later, after

he was long gone, that he gave our blue Persian carpet
to Franz Smetana who was broke and could sell it
for cash. He also gave money to his mother's seven
brothers and sisters, and some got out in time,
dispersing to Israel, Australia, South Africa. Or
the year he paid the bills for the Swiss sanitarium
my uncle stayed at after the war to put on fat. These
kindnesses, these things my father did without thinking
twice, what to say about them, about him? Except
that how a man treats his own children is only one
part of the story. And there are others.

MY FATHER'S MISTRESS

She of No Name

Maybe she wore sensible shoes, unlike our mother
of the high heels. Maybe she had a booming voice
and onions did not upset her stomach. I see freckles
and a pug nose, sky-blue eyes and flaxen hair, she
making him laugh with imitations of Peter Lorre
and Zsa Zsa Gabor. Maybe they met before the war,
fell madly in love, but forbidden to marry, so maybe
he merely settled for my mother who looked like
Gene Tierney, the most beautiful woman on earth
according to Darryl Zanuck. To my mother, looks
were everything and she worked hard at it, always
coiffed, always clean. Who knows what drove
my father to persist, summer after summer, checking
into the same Swiss sanitarium, he told us, to lose
weight, despite a wife who gave the best parties
in Forest Hills, served the best sachertorte off
the creamiest Limoges. Everyone ran circles
trying to please him. Who made him Lord of the table?

Herta

Then again, it could have been Herta Himmelreich
who lived in the Alps in a rustic chalet. We met her
one August, my sister and I, fresh from a month
at a Swiss boarding school where we were sent
to learn French, Herta, outdoorsy, cheerful, a wiz
in the kitchen, my mother and she greeting us
in dirndl skirts and peasant blouses, my father
all business, but maybe a touch too formal
with this woman who might have been his mistress. Surely
my mother would have noticed, unless her mind were
elsewhere, Mr. Himmelreich, perhaps, the two of them
flirting on the deck. There we were, my sister and I,
sullen, obedient, after a month of sneaking out at night
with the three daughters of King Farouk, to skinny
dip, sing dirty songs and blow smoke rings in the dark.

Lily

Had it been me, I would have chosen Lily Robinson
for her cigarette holders and thin Pall Malls, the only
one in the refugee circle who drew a beauty mark
next to her mouth, wore slinky black tuxedo pants
paired with a white satin blouse. She had the same air
as Marlene Dietrich only Lily's hair was black and shiny,
with razor sharp bangs and spit curls. Who wouldn't
have adored Lily, so devil-may-care, singing chansons
while husband Willy ran chords along the baby grand.
Rumor had it that there was a threesome, Lily, Willy
and Dodo, all three of them the best of friends. The rest
of the country loved Ozzie and Harriet, no wonder
I felt a world apart, where everyone here was because
of Hitler, everyone escaped while others had perished,
everyone took pills to bring on sleep, took marital risks,
drove too fast, favored sweets and could not get enough.

STAR

It was a silver star with the word *liar*
stamped on it and my father made me wear it
because I was one. He knew I hadn't taken
my bath, just turned the faucets on, knew
my scrapbook on Brazil was overdue (two
pictures of the Amazon pasted on the cover).
Spinning stories to wriggle out of things
made him madder, one deceit compounding
another, especially since my father was a man
of his word and his word was gold. I was glad
when he died and could let Danny feel me up

with no one the wiser, glad he didn't see me
run through his money like a woman bent
on ruination. If only he could have lied a little,
he who had so little charm, so little social grace.
But for him truth was absolute, was never gray.
As for me, there are so many truths it's hard
to tell the one big one that underlies them all:
I loved my father, love him even more today
though he was mean and cut me down to size
and I was small to begin with. He left me bare
of subterfuge without a leg to stand on but my own.

PRETTY STORIES, FUNNY PICTURES

When my mother dies I will not
visit her grave. No matter where
she makes her final bed, the plot
my father saved for her, or cramped

beside her beloved. She's already left
me my inheritance, those grisly tales
which steel the heart—*Struwwelpeter*
who lost his thumb, the one he sucked

(as I did mine) to the natty tailor
tiptoeing at night with giant shears.
Or the matchstick girl who refused
to eat and let her hair grow wild.

Ravens nested there. I was the obedient
child. But when she dies the truth
will out. I am her daughter. I won't
visit. I will be otherwise engaged.

WIEDERGUTMACHUNG

Fading, but still holding court
from bed, my mother last month received
a letter. For $18 a fund-finding agency
would trace "displaced" sums. She was sure
despite the late date, *Wiedergutmachungsgeld*
was coming her way, would "make good again"
her bitter bruises, mother gassed, father
in ashes, the violations of old age. So far

we hadn't seen a dime, though others
got more for losing less. Helga
for instance, $800 tax free per month
for life. But *Wiedergutmachung* never
was meant to pay for blood, only for what
a concrete number could be attached to—factory,
practice, butcher shop. On the tongue
the syllables sat dense, inert, like the potato

knödel we ate on Sundays. The house held other
pungencies: smoked liverwurst, headcheese made
of boiled hog parts floating in the vinegary
instability of aspic. Sometimes in spring
the knödel contained a sour cherry. Finally
$100 arrived from a defunct account. Since then
my mother dances, but only in dream. Like
the little mermaid, she is clumsy now on land, all

the senses dwindling. The milky scrim that dims
her sight, the front tooth that insists
on falling out. "Now I can't smile," she says
and hides her mouth, shy as a virgin. No loving
lips to kiss away the pain, no gold coins
tucked beneath her pillow. No sun-drenched
sailor to slip between the sheets where
she is waiting, in a nightgown, to be taken.

HOMEWORK

My father used to say
*If you've got nothing
to do, carry stones.*

In a sack, Father, I carry them

He said *If everyone jumped
in the lake, would you jump too?*

Yes, Father, the water is cool and green

If you're frightened of someone he said
imagine them in their underpants.

Father, I cannot even imagine your face

In the one snapshot of us
on the bridge in Baden Baden

the half smile on your lips is unfamiliar

You are standing behind me on a step
to make yourself taller, leaner

I am clutching my purse with both hands

And your hand on my shoulder—
it is heavy, Father, it is heavy

THE DAY BEFORE

The day before the war I dreamt you left me
for another woman, a native of your homeland
who grew up singing the same silly songs. Even
in my dream I knew you loved me still, but this
was different: like that time in Charlottesville
when we were guests pretending you were king
and I the royal baker's daughter.

The day before the war you dreamt that I was young
again, black bangs down to my eyebrows, my breasts pert
and impudent. It was fall and you weren't limping
yet, could've danced the fox trot had you so wished.
We were walking hand in hand, the leaves
already turned a fiery red.

The day the war broke out the TV switched
its focus, showed us billowing yellow clouds
and visions in green. It wasn't yet a week before
we learned that our supply lines were too thin
and we didn't have sufficient troops on the ground.
This wouldn't be the first time there were such
miscalculations: take you and me, the years
rolling over us like water, and us choking
on the dreams we once dreamed while awake.

FLIGHT

This morning, before any bird stirs, we rise
to a world without particulars, huddled

under covers of slate. By the time the first
tinge of pink stains the sky we are driving

untrafficked roads to the terminal where many
small surgeries are performed. Too soon

you sling your black satchel over your shoulder,
a traveler bound to a land sundered by rage.

I head back to town in my blue caravan
with only the shadow of heft, the echo of parry

and thrust. I see you squeezed in a narrow space,
oppressed by loss and the flesh of strangers.

In fact you are flying home via Zurich
and the cool remove of stewards in starched

shirts, the wilderness of your chest still fragrant
with the smell of sex. Tonight an unfettered

moon will graze terrains of our own forgetting.

FROM THE *BOOK OF JUDGES*

Once a Jew was defined as someone who always
carried a suitcase, his legacy a book and the clothes
on his back. And once this land was defined as a promise

of milk, a promise of honey. Now half-brothers fight for
a *dunam* of earth, a ceiling to count on. Now this land
is a promise gone haywire, a daredevil's mishap. Go out

in the street and play Russian roulette. Go out to a club
and find fresh young bodies blown to bits, their garments
still sparkling. Now the forest is burning. Charred skeletons

of trees provide neither food nor shelter. Goats grind
their teeth on whatever grows. Now the camera freezes
on demonstrators from both sides wearing baseball caps

and faded tee shirts, as though fitted by the same tailor
in a uniform of rage. Once these heights were volcanic—
the basalt rock remains look like ground pepper, or

stubble on a cheek. How to survive this place where
blood feuds last for eons, where sticks and stones
and absolutes reign and nothing, even sin, is original?

FAULT

Before God split the world into earth
and heaven, water was of one body, as before

Babel there was one tongue. *Shamayim*,
they say here, *there waters*, meaning *sky*.

We all live in terrible countries. Everywhere
people are rattled, perched at the lip of a great

divide. In the territories the air thickens while
over the Green Line armed guards patrol

maternity wings serving both Arab and Jew.
Last night I lost my footing in the dark. At noon

you tripped over a sand-camouflaged curb. This
was before the quake struck the rift running from

Cyprus to Syria. We didn't feel a thing, but the bees
went wild, sensing the shifts to which humans are dumb,

dive-bombing the trout smothered in date sauce,
your own bald pate, the world under the world.

BURNT OFFERING

Take your son
Which son
Your only son
They are both only
The one you love
I love them both
Isaac

—a Midrash

And he must have known while claving
the wood while honing the blade while
loading the ass and the long trek and
the pale sky steepening to madder red
there would be reprieve for he said *We*
to the two young men, *We will be back.*

Is it because at the feast I didn't
spare one turtledove, one fledgling

Under a scalding sun two tamarisks
shimmer, bound to their shadows.
Two tamarisks, their calcine buds
shriveled into little white corpses.

As if a tree could offer the sun
return for what entered the leaf

Drenched in sweat, forehead pressed
to a flat rock at the lip of Moriah
nostrils inhaling an acrid smell
that was not unpleasing, of fat.

And always the sensation
of being watched

At the edge. His whole body gripped
by vertigo, an urge to hurl himself
down into his former life where
two boys sport around the kindling fire
pitching broom twigs into the flames
to make them flare, the wild one, oh
beloved Ishmael, and the one who is fair.

SARAH REFLECTS

I like to watch him use the knife,
wield the blade just so the rind

falls away in segments, leaving
the shivering fruit. It shows

his hand knows when to stop
and when to let go. So when he pines

again for the other woman it comes
as the blade comes, swift

precision. I could have made
my exit then, transformed myself

into penumbra. I could have
but didn't, chose instead to step

into the world of whir and muck,
the stuff of the daily. First birth

then death, the grand finale,
and in between, the well-honed

knife, the glistening fruit, and all
the major and minor incisions.

MILCAH

Escape for thy life; look not behind thee...
—Gen. 19.17

I called her Milcah and she was mine.
As my two daughters never were, but
from the start belonged to him, the way
he fondled them, their corkscrew curls.

You must sing to goats and they will come,
faster if you sing their name. Milcah came
to me as I came to my mother, unbidden.
She let down her milk for me alone.

All goats bleat and I know them all
by their bleat, as God knows us by
a turn of phrase, or the way we bow
our heads. That day an unnatural shriek

I thought was fear, for the land had grown
strangely dark, as if the sun had shrouded
herself in a muddy *kutonet*. I raced
to the far pasture to find Milcah trapped

between two fields, her horns and neck
caught beneath a fence. She turned, sensing
my approach. And then the crack. They
dragged me away, the girls, their arms

sheathed with silver bangles. The sound
of little bells. The mules straining under
their load of barley, flagons of wine, crushed
spices. But Milcah trapped between two fields,

her lovely horns, her neck. You must bury
the dead else they will rise. If you do not
turn toward what you are twined to
you are not fit to walk this earth.

DYBBUK

Some bodies are washed and wrapped in white linen
then placed, coffinless, underground. Others fall
into ditches, heaped over layers of bone. No matter

how, spirits do not settle down, but rise in our throats
speaking in voices we know: *Beware the dark one.*
Collect what is owed. Keep the knives honed. We are

as one transfixed, chin tilted skyward, traces of salt
on forehead and cheek. They could depart from
window or door or the little toe of the left foot, if

they wished. They do not wish. They poke and prod,
insist. We call in the troops, the exorcists. Somewhere
to the east pocked walls reek of holy oil and garlic, troughs

overflow with that which must not be eaten. It is April
and nothing is growing. Generation unto generation
we are riven. By the dead grinding their grief. Let us

prepare for them an offering: broth of brine and sprig
of laurel. Perhaps then they will rest easy, won't
raise such a ruckus and pillage the larder, mad for feed.

NAMING A CITY

Madame Carcas said *feed the pig* she said
now heave it over the ramparts. It sailed pinkly
through the parched air, guts splattering
when it touched earth. Troops gathered round
considering the undigested grain. Surely
the siege had failed if there was food enough
to waste on pigs. Surely they had miscalculated
and it was they who would eat dust, rations
already diminished, an enflamed moon foretelling
winter. They broke camp and left.
$\qquad\qquad\qquad\qquad\qquad$ Saved. Inside
the walls, cheers, great joy. And then the ringing
of bells, the sonorous chimes. *Carcassonne*. This
is how the city was named. And now a carousel
and a yellow train. We marvel and pay up. As though
it was long ago. As though there will always be summer
and women seasoned enough to keep us from starving.

PRODUITS DE TERROIR

This is not another travel poem, although I could go on
about the bluffs, massive in their verticality, or the river
snaking through the gorge, dark and green as the devil's
throat, how the women are bony and thinlipped, their men
more accustomed to judging than being judged. But no,
this is of the dreams we have when we are far from home—
for seven days now—and feeling foreign to ourselves.
In yours we're armed with skillet and Swiss army knife
outnumbered by a band of two-bit thugs. For me
it's Grand Central Station and there's a war on, tanks
and bombs and me running, one shoe on, one shoe off.
Wherever we go terror follows, its yellow eyes piercing
sleep. And stalks us by day: at the market local sausage
and cheese called "produits de terroir." Terror
has always been with us, in the garden with its chaos
of rocks, the sun turning its face, waters rising, blood
of dogs, starvation, cholera, nights when we were cold
and alone, when trains ran on the dot.

CONSERVATOR

Handling the uniforms doesn't bother me, what grates is no sense
of urgency, the standing around. Well, the smaller ones got to me
at first, they still do, because these were worn by children. Sometimes

I treat one that's made a little different, a little nicer, maybe an inside
pocket, because of a bribe, or a little extra food. Or triangular inserts
sewn in the pants of former prisoners, who marched in annual parades

and over the years, put on weight. There are those with shoulder
pads, from later, for musicians in the orchestra, invited often
after the War to perform. The same blue and gray coarse material

but tailored like a suit. What bothers me is no one knowing anything
about the period. If I hadn't haggled with the gypsies, it would have
been no one. We spoke the same language, had the same nose

for forgery, fabric rubbed with coffee grounds, the tannin stains
passed off as dirt, the color of the stars all wrong. It's not so bad
to work down here, in the basement, with white noise leaking out

from the machine room, low humidity, and lamps that make it seem
it's always daylight, the sun, always shining. Of course, I'd prefer
preserving beauty, but this pays better, and I still get to use my craft.

HEADQUARTERS

I have been sitting in this chair, this office, this
room with a window that doesn't open so long
I fear I've lost the art of breathing. My task is

to draft speeches for powerful people that must pass
through the eyes of a man scared of losing his job.
The trick is to write in his style so he can get

the credit. In this way I become indispensable. Strange
how common ghosting is. Today I heard my own
words coming from the chief of staff, exhorting us

to *soften the environment for brand acceptance*, bombard
it with the message that this association is *new and
innovative*, helping people over 50 enjoy life. I am

over 50 and not enjoying life. Perhaps because
I've strayed from my own nature. *Traditore*, traitor,
doctor of spin, me whose aim is clarity, telling it

slant. Sometimes I almost feel at home here, and here
is east of Eden, downtown on the Red Line, wellfed,
wellgroomed, making a killing in the Land of Nod.

RIDDLE

Real, mean, a stitch in,
any way you cut it, you're in it,
up to your gills in it, you rise
in it and sink, that great leveler,
you kill it, live on borrowed tock
and tick, once upon a it
begins and then goes by as I
will love you till the end of it.

FORTUNE'S DARLING

Spitting Image
Born with a cowlick, a black tuft untamed
by cradlesong. Blessed with two deft hands
and a flair for forgery. Underlings stack
the flatware, prop the rickety staircase,
prepare the borscht. Not she of the four
crinolines, the seven silk scarves. Sloe-eyed
in the casino of chance, she croons her come-ons
to runaway Jacks and reins them in. Grooms
them with a devious tongue, a red-hot brush.
The bridle, the whip, attuned and insomniac.

Her Four Crinolines
One for each husband, the first with a tick
and eyebrows that jittered, supplanted by he
who overparslied soup. The third spun tales
garnished with rue and the fourth had a gift
for naming the townlets encircling her waist.
Each husband—the restless, the green, the glum
and exact—beheld, abandoned, eventually
turned to fluted layers of taffeta and bone
concealing her own ample hips from the time
black-mascaraed lashes flutter, then blink.

Souvenir
Once the sun slides down from the trees
they ask about that scar next to her lip.
(Curiosity? Envy?) "Rose petal to ward off
melancholia," she says, or "the swishing tail
of a horse," or "a happenstance." What she aims
for is far out of range, like yesterday's harbor
from a bird's eye view, a perspective found
in certain Dutch landscapes and later filched
by Italian masters. How fibs bring home
foreign vistas. Talismen cooked to perfection.

What She Eats

Fated to be fickle in food as in love. Not
one flavor that she craves but a lick of this,
of that. Sauerkraut and caraway, pickled
beets, mutton and leeks. This does not even
touch upon the subject of sweets, for her
nonnegotiable, as for others, faith. She takes
her lumps of sugar straight. Or with crushed
poppyseed to make a paste. Dusted over
dumplings, powdered over cake. Never having
swilled mother's milk, nutmeg in her coffee, black.

Cameo of Fortune

About her, what can one say? That after
birth she lost no time losing weight.
The earliest memory is of her stepping out
sporting red patent-leather pumps, the heels,
spiked. Upon return, she'd pose fullface
before the hallway mirror, remove the stickpin
from her hunter-green felt beret. "Did anyone
call?" she'd ask and pat Darling's ginger curls
much the way one strokes a cat. About her
what's the most one can say? That she returned.

Those Nights

Fortune grew old, her hip joints frozen.
Grew meanspirited to Darling who didn't
come, didn't care, didn't do enough, why
should she leave her anything? At the end
she willed her shoes (which fit) and green
felt hat and after that her own shroud
of breath became oppressive. Those nights
she fought sleep like drowning, lungs pinched
and starved for air. Those nights when air
was everything, capacious and uplifting.

Wee One

She slipped into this world as fearlessly as fish
leap. One breath, the rapids breached. Darling
wept, sodden with love. Everything dissolved
into *we* and *us*, the present conjugated more
expansively. Then there was the Jack the child
called *dat* who hung around fixing things. No
kitchen faucets springing leaks or light bulbs out
of reach. Winter they planted hyacinths, spring
they bloomed and summer greened and fall fell and
winter they planted—Fortune's Darling's darling.

The Way She Likes It

She wears her fortune lightly as a thin scrim
of ice on a clear window pane. Which can be
cracked at the faintest tap. A wren's beak, say,
or a squirrel's claw. Add a cat's lapping tongue.
As can happen any time, any place. Where she is
right now? At the precipice of morning, where
nothing is in place and all is nascent and undone.
Just the way she likes it, she to whom decision
means cutting off, cutting out, diminution of
the possible, the *that* that we can never fathom.

ELEMENTALS

I know numbers are beautiful. If they aren't, nothing is.
—Paul Erdos, *The Man Who Loved Only Number.*

In this house everything happens and weather
is always extreme: hail and snow and today
a storm rolling in with phantom smells—bacon

burning, dough rising. Nothing is burning or
rising unless it's the past and how to perceive it.
Like where to stow away phantoms, those toeless

ghosts and the pain that radiates from what is
no longer there. Which is worse: A damaged
parietal lobe, or amputation? Mother in limbo

in bed, or Father's exacting standards confounding
the grave? What do we have but a house that needs
furnishing. Start with design, handknotted, one

of a kind. Beauty at the mercy of minors, a minimal
wage. A famous mathematician called children *epsilons*,
the Greek letter signifying small quantities. Instead

of a chimney a tower of digits, the company of primes
to stave off sensation. He penned his own epitaph: *At last
I shall grow stupider no more.* Not humility. A cut above.

AMULET

May the Lord of Death pass over
this house. May the Lord of Envy
not curdle our whey. May the Lord
of Greed release us from craving.
Great Lord of Time, grant us a stay.

FAIRYTALE

Once upon a time
a baby boy was born
to a suicidal woman
and a suicidal man.

He was not born to make her sane
nor to help the marriage last
but because his birth would save
his daddy from the draft.

The war has come and gone,
the dead lie in its wake:
he put a bullet in his head,
she drowned in Crystal Lake.

The little boy is now a man
and takes himself a wife.
One hand gently strokes her hair,
the other strokes his knife.

FLOCK

The Lord is my shepherd
He rides a red tractor
His work boots caked
With earth and dried dung

He leadeth His sheep
Beside the green pastures
His black dog yapping
To keep them in line

They bow their heads down
To nibble the clover
And lap still waters
They do not want

Nor fear any evil
Grazing in shadows
Their guttural baahs
Akin to amen

WEIGHT

In a small village not very
long ago, rats were summoned
to court and when they failed
to appear they were found
not guilty by virtue of cats
and crows who would have gnawed
their bones had they obliged.

*

After the fair closed down
around ten, we went back
to buy two blackmarket chickens—
one with golden coloration,
the other with feathers like
herringbone tweed. No brooding
on eggs stolen from others.

*

The pallbearers took turns carrying
the casket. To the south lay
the sea, and north, the castle
and beyond the stone was the maiden
Margot whose yeast cakes were always
studded with raisins. How heavy
death is if you don't take turns.

FAR-FLUNG

Honeybees and frogs are fast disappearing. What
will become of little green apples, the loneliness
of lilypads? Some species of moths no longer pollinate
Arizonan yuccas. Askance, askew, something is
amiss. A tsunami one hundred feet high washes away
three thousand souls in Papua, New Guinea. It's hard
to know when disasters are natural. Once I was stung
by a bee and my arm swelled like a melon. In college
a date slipped a frog down my blouse and I couldn't
stop screaming, those frantic hind legs. In high school
I pithed a toad. Later I saw a half-carved cadaver, head
and feet wrapped in soaked cloth, the yellow jelly we
call fat. The leaner they are, the harder to cut. Blanding's
turtles don't deteriorate with age. Our brain is the size
of two clenched fists. The hand is the most complicated
of organs. Which, as is written on a card I carry
in my wallet, I will donate to others—eyes, liver, lungs,
heart, whatever can be salvaged, should all else fail.

THE FULLNESS THEREOF

The earth is the Lord's, and the fullness thereof; the world,
and they that dwell therein.
                                        —Psalm 24

i

In the beginning a riot of color, burnt umber, magenta,
madder red. Vast expanses of indigo. There was thunder
and the absence of thunder. There was heat, earth shifting,
hills swelling, ridges rising. Then came the fingerlings,
the frogs and dark-eyed juncos. Possum and hawk
and fox. There were buffalo, mountain lions. There were
slender legs of spiders and dragonflies. Mosquitoes trapped
on salmon-colored salamanders' flickering tongues. Black
bears lumbering through the underbrush. Speckled eggs,
beavers, fire ants. Night crawlers wriggling below, crows
cawing above, there was earth and the fullness thereof.

ii

We forded the river, the one named Euphrates, the highest
mountain, we called it Mount George, the one we crossed
over, Mount Spotswood. We numbered the trout and muskie,
the brooks they swam in. We tracked all species of fowl.
We blazed trails in the forest and left distinguishing marks.
The winnowing down of daylight, that was good. Once
two geese swooped in. He swam up and down the pond
fixing his amber eye on me. She tucked her head beneath
one wing. Stars were our faithful companions and we drank
to their health, as we did to the King and the rest of the Royal
Family. In this way we cleared the path to today.

iii

It's hard to think of home without the hawthorn and the scat
of deer and mole. It's hard to think of fall without the sight
of scurrying squirrels packing nuts into their cheeks, fearing
humans less than winter. It's hard to think of me without my
hound, my hound, heaven's staunchest ally. It's hard to live
on this land without hearing sounds of all sorts of creatures, all
digging out towards light, or burrowing within, breathing deeply
of the darkening night. To love a place is to love where you are,
to know it is beyond compare, the air, the scent, it might as well
be skin, it is to touch, be touched by everything in the surround,
to feel at one yet fully other in this diverse dominion.

GOURMAND'S PRAYER

Yellowtail snapper with citrus beurre blanc, filet
mignon in demi-glace cabernet, roast duck garnished
with mint jellied peaches, angels on horseback—dates
stuffed with garlic cloves wrapped in bacon and served
in a hot honey-pepper sauce, bananas foster, key
lime pie, dense, flourless chocolate cake drizzled
with a raspberry coulis, Lord, grant me the power
to well digest all that I have well eaten.

from

Kingdom of Speculation

(2015)

THE KINGDOM OF SPECULATION

Eggs coddled or poached are the food
of choice in the Kingdom of Speculation

for eggs are exceedingly rare and stored
in brooders. Brooders are guarded by men

who sport checkered vests and twirl
batons. To steal an egg is to be beaten

to death and the graves of thieves
are stacked like dominoes at the edge

of town. The rich feast on eggs
while the poor eat dumplings which look

like eggs but sink in the belly. Chickens
are revered, the most popular tunes

being hymns composed in their honor.
In this Kingdom only the weather is fair

and the air holds the scent of cardamom.
Overhead birds fly ignored, singing

an ostinato: *what if, what if, what if*

THE BLOOD OF A KING

Once there was a certain King who pricked
his thumb on the thorn of a white rose.
Even the blood of a King runs scarlet, and did.

It ran and ran. It ran until all the rivers
and streams in the Kingdom ran red. Then
the fields turned red and everything that grew

in them, corn, barley, soon the milk from the cows
and goats. And when the Princess wept for her father
her tears ran red. And then he died. He was buried

without pomp in the red earth, leaving
the Kingdom in disarray—the Queen
took to muscatel and her royal bed, attended

by seven simpering knaves. The Minister of Finance
retired to the counting house to count up the money.
There was plenty. He issued an edict forthwith

forbidding the pleasures of hunting, dancing, racing
and conversing, then galloped by horseback out
of the Kingdom, followed by a pack of 42 mules

hauling coffers of sovereigns. And thus
the wealth of the Kingdom was carted away.
The Kingdom languished under a shroud of thirst

and silence. But over time a particular flower
thrived, which the Princess, a botanist, named
amaranthus caudatus, love-lies-bleeding.

THREE CASKETS

A Princess with three suitors finds them all
lacking: casket of silver, casket of gold,
casket of lead. She considers lead—

he's heavy. If she ties herself to him
she'll sink. But oh the liquefaction
of sheets, and oh wouldn't she expire

in the rapture of that deep. Silver
flashes slick off the tundra, elusive
as flight. In his wake, a killing

freeze, an excess of courtesy. At first
gold's glitter dazzles, his overflowing
pockets. Fortuna is his mother, but

his expression's a trifle stupid. How's
a Princess to rule with no casket
for her jewels? At this hour the shops

are closed. The graveyard beckons
but the coffins are sealed with old
remains. She's been here before,

her legacy these ruby scars, those
smoky pearls. Let her string them
on a flaxen thread for all to see.

Let them incite the mercy of thieves.
Let her step forth in the ancestral land
accompanied by her two royal hands.

SLOUGH OF THE SEVEN TOADS

The elation of naming, that dispassionate
stance, of course it could not last. As all

first steps it was bound to lead to that first
misstep, that attenuated fall through ebony

branches into the Forest of Indifference. Oh
how to define the pain of it, the eclipse

of sky, the scales that seemed to sprout
over her eyes, the petals of love-lies-bleeding

wilting in that thicket of night? Then a headlong
plunge into the slough of the seven toads

and there defiled by false iridescence, the barter,
the intrigue, the back and forth, that rough

exchange, the petty puffery of fame,
the flat inspection of their malachite eyes.

THE HIGHWAY OF BONES

Under no stars on the highway
of bones, the Princess broods

on her losses: the King is dead,
the Queen is dead, her beloved

nursemaid Gertruda demented, she
who spun fanciful tales of dwarfs

with spurs on their boots. Farewell
Gertruda. Thus intent, the Princess

trips on a femur, falls, cracks open
her head. Demons appear to snatch

that part of her soul called *memoria*.
Out flies the King, the Queen, Gertruda,

and everything she ever knew, that one
and one makes two, that two from two

is naught. And there she might lie
till this very day had her shadow not

lassoed the demons with a skein
of dreams, thus releasing memoria

which recomposed in the Princess's
skull, who awoke, remembered, refreshed.

THE BARKER'S CALL

The moon had slipped down in the sky
when the Minister of Finance sneaked back
to the Kingdom of Speculation. There

he dismounted and following the barker's
call, wagered all on the contest between
Reason and Passion. Reason was splendid

in spangled tights, flexing his fabulous
biceps. The Minister promptly lost
his heart. Passion, that kleptomaniac,

stunned him with her ardent gaze, her
see-through frou frou. She stole
his breath away. Finding himself

with no heart or breath, the Minister
expired on the spot, not even his pack
of mules or their cargo could save him.

TWO MANGLED HEAPS

Noon in the Kingdom. The sun
fixes its steady gaze on Reason

and Passion, two mangled heaps
on the floor. They gingerly rise,

bones aching from lying so
fiercely entwined, then wend

their way to a sequestered inn.
This is where they hold their secret

rendezvous, where they kiss and
make up, tending to each other's

wounds, as they are wont to do.

THE EARLY CHILDHOOD OF GRIEF

And from the loins of Reason and Passion
springs Grief, a surly, birdlike boy

who refuses to cry. No gurgling, no babbling,
no scattershot foray into the dense

and dissonant world, choosing instead
to stay mute, to absorb it all

through his eyes, his parents, their singular
deadlock. Passion has no patience

for Grief, nor Reason, the stomach,
so consumed are they by each other.

Grief grows in time as time grows
in him, each nanosecond adding

to his girth. Soon he's wearing
a polka dot vest on his way to school

where he loses his marbles, is pelted
with dumplings. He finds refuge lying

flat on his back in an open field
where he studies the sky, the inhabitants

thereof, at ease in that recitative,
consoled by the heavenly undertones.

NO SMALL FEAT

No small feat for Grief to doff
his mourning cloak, the velvet
heft of it, and its scarlet naught

emblazoned in cross stitches, insignia
for *not enough*. He might easily
have kept it on, remaining wrapped

in sorrow, for surely there is enough
sorrow in this world to dwell in. If we
could earn a crown for every soul

we found shrouded in despair, why
we'd be richer than a dozen kings!
Which explains why moths grow fat

and tailors are by nature cheerful,
day in, day out, their nimble fingers
stitching habits of our own choosing.

THE MASTER OF CHANCE

The Princess looking no more
like a Princess than you or I
lifted one shabby foot over

the border into the Province
of Chance. And there
was accosted by a hard-boiled

brooder. Oh he was chic, very chic
indeed, with gleaming spats, pomaded
mustache and a voice that was pure

basso profundo. *Dear Madam*, he purred,
I am Rodrigo, the Master of Chance. Be
my bride. Polish my coffer, keep

count of my chickens. The Princess,
as you must know by now, was no fool
and recognized a casket of gold

when she saw one. To be the wife
of a brooder held no appeal, but yes,
she wanted to see the coffer, and when

she did, knew it at once for the one
belonging to her father. The brooder,
watching her stroke the coffer, told

how a gambling man lost it to Passion,
A woman in my employ, as is everyone
in this State, for I'm the Master

of Chance, I cut the deck, declare
what's wild, as you are my dear, my Balkis,
my Hatshepsut, my true Queen of Hearts.

SMALL WONDER

The Master of Chance is the only master
in the Kingdom of Speculation, sole keeper
of odds, of track, of coffers. Three cheers

for the Master, his fine mustache! All Hail
Rodrigo's Formulation: probability equals
N/(p-n). His subjects have it engraved

on their foreheads, bow down in awe. Yet
Rodrigo is barred from the carriage where travel
Deep Conviction, Absolute Certainty, and that

crusty crusader, Crux of the Matter. Who merely
pass through this way on their way somewhere
else, and each in a first-class compartment.

It rankles. Snubbed as master non grata.
Even a blind boy who aims at a hawk can
sometimes by Chance manage a hit. Small

wonder he finds the Princess enchanting.
She brings the blood to his chilly cheeks,
a fact for which there is no accounting.

THE NATURE OF NATURE

After debating the nature of nature
over a pipe and a demitasse, after

helping the Princess sort through her
satchel, its slapdash array of botanical

specimens, Reason pries off the lid
of the coffer, using two thumbs. Alas!

one whiff of the rotting eggs and the two
collapse in a swoon. Six ravens descend,

celestial consorts of the dead, six ravens
who peck at all the eggs save one, the ivory

Egg of Perfection, which cannot be cracked.

A GREAT DARKNESS FALLS

What the Princess can't guess is that Deep
Conviction in fact has convened such a Congress
where Chance pops up, an unexpected

guest. In time the Princess arrives
with the King's coffer, a fertile bed
for her cuttings and seeds. Inside

her purse, the Egg of Perfection, her ticket
home, price for safe passage. A mighty wind
whips through the castle extinguishing

light. Confusion ensues—the Princess
falls into the arms of Deep Conviction
while Chance, that fickle cavalier, fumbles

for Absolute Certainty, wild for her
creamy complexion, her dainty neck.
Crux takes a shine to the tender

lad Compassion. All is poised for
an *ever after*. Sing praise to the Great
Lord Chaos, his enabling dark. Praise

to the touch of a choice companion.
And praise to the Egg of Perfection
glowing in the folds of a lady's purse.

ABOUT THE AUTHOR

Barbara Goldberg grew up Forest Hills, New York, in a German-speaking household of Holocaust survivors. Her father, mother, grandmother, and infant sister, along with 30,000 other refugees on the run from the Nazis, received Portuguese visas from Aristides de Sousa Mendes, the Portuguese counsel in Bordeaux, France, during World War II. These visas allowed her family safe passage through Spain to Lisbon, where they boarded a ship bound for New York. Goldberg is the first member of her family born in the United States.

After graduating Phi Beta Kappa in philosophy at Mount Holyoke College, Goldberg went on for an MEd at Columbia University and an MFA at American University. In her career as a speechwriter, Goldberg wrote radio scripts for CBS News correspondent Harry Reasoner, among others.

The author of five prize-winning books of poetry, including the Felix Pollak Prize in Poetry for *The Royal Baker's Daughter*, Goldberg also translates from French and from the Hebrew, including *Scorched by the Sun*, poems by Israeli poet Moshe Dor. Goldberg and Dor co-translated and edited *The Fire Stays in Red: Poems by Ronny Someck* as well as four anthologies of contemporary Israeli poetry, including *After the First Rain: Israeli Poems of War and Peace*, and *The Stones Remember*, which received an award from the Witter Bynner Foundation.

The recipient of two fellowships from the National Endowment for the Arts, numerous grants from the Maryland State Arts Council, as well as national awards in translation, fiction and speechwriting, Goldberg is Series Editor of The Word Works International Editions, having curated and edited volumes translated from many languages, including Ancient Greek, Kurdish, French, and Croatian.

ABOUT THE WORD WORKS

Since its founding in 1974, The Word Works has steadily published volumes of contemporary poetry and presented public programs. Its imprints include The Washington Prize, The Tenth Gate Prize, The Hilary Tham Capital Collection, and International Editions.

Monthly, The Word Works offers free literary programs in the Chevy Chase, MD, Café Muse series, and each summer it holds free poetry programs in Washington, D. C.'s Rock Creek Park. Word Works programs have included "In the Shadow of the Capitol," a symposium and archival project on the African American intellectual community in segregated Washington, D.C.; the Gunston Arts Center Poetry Series; the Poet Editor panel discussions at The Writer's Center; Master Class workshops; and a writing retreat in Tuscany, Italy.

As a 501(c)3 organization, The Word Works has received awards from the National Endowment for the Arts, the National Endowment for the Humanities, the D.C. Commission on the Arts & Humanities, the Witter Bynner Foundation, Poets & Writers, The Writer's Center, Bell Atlantic, the David G. Taft Foundation, and others, including many generous private patrons.

An archive of artistic and administrative materials in the Washington Writing Archive is housed in the George Washington University Gelman Library. The Word Works is a member of the Community of Literary Magazines and Presses and its books are distributed by Small Press Distribution.

❧ wordworksbooks.org ❧

OTHER WORD WORKS BOOKS

Annik Adey-Babinski, *Okay Cool No Smoking Love Pony*
Karren L. Alenier, *Wandering on the Outside*
Andrea Carter Brown, *September 12*
Christopher Bursk, ed., *Cool Fire*
Willa Carroll, *Nerve Chorus*
Grace Cavalieri, *Creature Comforts*
Abby Chew, *A Bear Approaches From the Sky*
Nadia Colburn, *The High Shelf*
Henry Crawford, *Binary Planet*
Barbara Goldberg, *Berta Broadfoot and Pepin the Short*
Akua Lezli Hope, *Them Gone*
Frannie Lindsay, *If Mercy*
Elaine Magarrell, *The Madness of Chefs*
Chloe Martinez, *Ten Thousand Selves*
Marilyn McCabe, *Glass Factory*
JoAnne McFarland, *Identifying the Body*
Leslie McGrath, *Feminists Are Passing From Our Lives*
Kevin McLellan, *Ornitheology*
Anatoly Molotkov, *Future Symptoms*
Ann Pelletier, *Letter That Never*
W.T. Pfefferle, *My Coolest Shirt*
Ayaz Pirani, *Happy You Are Here*
Robert Sargent, *Aspects of a Southern Story*
      & *A Woman From Memphis*
Julia Story, *Spinster for Hire*
Cheryl Clark Vermeulen, *They Can Take It Out*
Julie Marie Wade, *Skirted*
Miles Waggener, *Superstition Freeway*
Fritz Ward, *Tsunami Diorama*
Camille-Yvette Welsh, *The Four Ugliest Children in Christendom*
Amber West, *Hen & God*
Maceo Whitaker, *Narco Farm*
Nancy White, ed., *Word for Word*

ꙮ *For a complete list of our available books, visit our website!* ꙮ